UnNormal

Faith Allison

UnNormal / Faith Allison Mascato

In my life, the loss of my mother at birth deeply impacted me. Yet, the discovery of her pride in me as I describe to you in this book truly healed me of so much. As such, I dedicate this book to Betty Lorraine Treutle. Thank you for carrying me so faithfully in your womb and naming me from the heart of God. Your inheritance in me has dividends paying off to your reward. I can't wait to meet you in person some day!

CONTENTS

ACKNOWLEDGEMENTS

I first want to acknowledge my daughter Brandi Lynn Ginty, whose professional services at Inkible.co have truly helped me be better at my craft. I also want to thank you for not holding my past against me and daring to be amazing, despite it all! I am so proud of who you are!

I also want to acknowledge the spiritual parents I have been blessed to do life with. Thank you to John and Lisa Carter, Irene Morgan, Annie Rowland, Kelly and Gina Lynnes, Burnard and Jessie Scott, Chris and Margie Scarinzi, Robert and Jean Tringale. Your wisdom, love and the opportunities you gave me to be with you have helped to shape my life.

Lastly, I want to thank my friend Neal Carsten who first demonstrated the unconditional love of God to me. Though you are with the Lord, I know you are cheering me on from the grandstands of heaven. This one too, goes to your account. I am forever grateful to you for seeing, knowing and loving me.

FOREWORD

A prophetic word that comes from God will truly have its way when it is released on the Earth. Such was the word that I received from Prophet Andre Brockhorst in April of 2020. I share it with you to demonstrate that though it was a recent word for me, it contained the revelation of many previous prophetic words I had received in the past. However, this time, it brought understanding with it. I began to become *me* – more completely *me* than ever before – as that word settled into me and opened itself up. Here it is:

> *It seems to me, Faith that God is bringing order to your life. You are in one place; your heart is in a different place and your mind is in another place. You are all over the place, all over the world. And God is bringing order and stability to that. Not that its wrong or you have missing anything wrong but that there are many things God has put in your heart and there are things you need to finish; a season needs to end. Stuff of the past, Things you were busy with, captured by, a book is closing and the documents of that season are - a couple of things - God has ended and those documents need to be finished. God is closing a specific season in your life and ending it for*

once and for all and then God is birthing new season of new things God has for you.

You have to know; you are a global citizen. Not just in America, one nation or one place but God has called you to make an impact in the world. Not just one nation. Your hands are stretched out to the globe. God has called you and God is preparing you to have an impact globally. God has called you have an impact in Europe. A tremendous impact in Europe. I sense God is connecting you to someone in Europe... Switzerland. A lady, same age, same circumstances, situation. So, God is opening a door, making a connection to someone in Europe. You are going to have a big impact in Europe. And not just there but globally.

Continue to prepare and get ready. God will create the platform for you to be able to do that.

Your eyes will see the truth, not what people have for you but what God has for you. People will do and be for us because they love us and want to protect us. But God is our protector and God is our source. And God has big dreams and big ideas about us. They have your best interest in mind but it is your life is not about what is safe or what is within bounds. You are called to be a boundary breaker, to break boundaries all over the place. You are called to go above what has been done or what people think is normal.

You are not normal and there is not one thing normal about you. You are called to live a different life than other people. So, to them certain things might be the normal way of living and doing things. You are not called to be normal. You are called to live the life that God has for you to live. For many years you have been limited in your life to do what God has called you to do, but at last, right now, you are in a stage of life now where there's absolutely nothing that is limiting you from what God has called you to do or holding you back. And God's not going to allow anything to come in and hold you back again. He is not going to allow any weights to come back in and hold down or drown you. It's very important for His Kingdom to be built globally... There are areas that God is opening up to you. Over time there are areas that God is opening up to you and over time you will see how it opens. I see small little doors all over Europe and all over the world opening to you, I see Russia. All these places all over with doors opening up to you one after the other. And it's not about God pushing us so hard as to break us, but God is opening doors up for you all over as you can go forth. And you can handle it. And He is going to send you. The purpose is not to exhaust you and run you dry but to use you effectively for His Kingdom globally. And so, I sense God is going to do an effective work through your life and in the kingdom globally.

Prophet Andre Brockhorst, South Africa

INTRODUCTION

In 1953, a young Christian woman named Betty married the man she had fallen deeply in love with. His name was Billy. Betty had dreamed of marriage and family. Billy was a widower and had three boys to whom Betty had become another mother. Once they married, she had a daughter two years later and then another two years after that. Her life was filled with mothering, baking, and making a home for her children. Her home was "the place to be" for all her children's friends. The smell of fresh baked snickerdoodles and the soft touch of a mother were always in abundance for every child that entered that home.

Giving birth was not an easy thing for Betty. She had a mild heart defect and the stress of the difficult labor for each child took a toll on her body. She was advised by her doctor to never get pregnant again after the birth of her second child. Her desire to be a mother was strong and she did not heed his advice.

Six years later and pregnant again, she suffered a miscarriage. The doctor's concerns were very real to her then, but she still did not share what he had told her with her family. She didn't want to worry them. When she found herself pregnant again 4 years later, she rejoiced even while she squelched the fear in her own heart. As she grew heavy with the child she carried and felt her body becoming unnaturally tired, she knew something might not be right with her, but she trusted God and so longed for this baby that she tried to just push through. Her prayers were fiercely protective of this child. "This one I will not lose," she thought.

The day her baby was born full-term, as the labor started, she kissed her girls goodbye and told them she would be home soon with their baby sister. Almost two days later, Billy came home without Betty. He faced the difficult task of telling his family that their mother had passed. Though the baby had survived the birth, her mother had slipped away the very next day. Her heart had failed her and she passed without even having the opportunity to hold the baby girl she had fought so hard to live for. Somehow now, Billy would have to figure out how to care for his young girls who had lost their mother.

The overwhelming grief that enveloped him every time he looked at that baby girl was difficult for Billy to bear. That little girl grew up through many family transitions and during most of the formative years of her life, she felt lost and uncared for. She often felt a deep anger towards her from her father that seemed irrational to her. She learned to care for herself, how to hide and avoid pain, and how to recover from wounds afflicted by others. The young woman grew up with one overwhelmingly strong belief: *Not much in life is safe or dependable.* A voice in her soul whispered always, "You are the only one whom you can depend on."

With this belief, she developed a core life skill that served her well - the ability to pull herself up by her bootstraps. There was no mess she got into, no wound inflicted upon her, no betrayal so deep that she could not survive by pulling herself up and out of it each and every time. There was only one problem with this. It was hard to maintain. It wore deeply on her soul and made her body sick. Her habits of self-care centered around comforting herself with other things, and this weighed deeply on her, never truly satisfying with any lasting power.

Here's the problem she faced. She had been birthed into this world at a great cost and given a name that would speak into her destiny. This ghostly feeling of greatness and destiny seemed often like a bad dream to her. Every time she settled into another relationship, job or identity; they would fail to be a perfect fit. She often felt chameleon-like, adjusting her life and identity around others. She wanted desperately to be seen. She wanted her own mother. She feared her father. Her name seemed like a curse.

You see, in the hours after Betty gave birth, while she and Billy faced the reality that she may not survive the next day, she had one request – to name her baby girl. Billy disagreed with the name she wanted and felt that filling out the birth certificate was not as essential as going home to get his girls and return to the hospital. When Billy left her for a short period of time, Betty asked the nurse to bring her the birth certificate. She filled out her baby girl's name and signed the certificate. She handed it back to the nurse after extracting a promise to keep it safe until she was gone. Only then could her husband sign it, as well. She passed on before Billy even returned back to the hospital.

The next day as Billy left for home with a baby girl in his arms and a funeral to plan for his beloved wife, the nurses gave him the baby's certificate to sign. He discovered then that Betty's last wish was granted. Her baby girl was to be called *Faith Allison*.

Yes, that baby Billy held in his arms was me. That story is mine. That name would speak over me every time someone called for me. It was not a curse. It was a promise God had released with a purpose into the Earth through a little girl whose faith life could change an entire generation. Each time someone called me by name, the voice of that promise beckoned in the midst of the other voices, experiences, and labels assigned to me by others.

My mother's last act was prophetic. The word of the Lord through her was determined to have its way and it would run like a bulldozer at times through the carefully laid structures of my life, creating space and room for God's purpose to be made known. I have come to know it well. I want to share that journey with you in the hopes that you will find a compelling sense of destiny calling to you, beyond the voices of others. May God's voice be activated and run swiftly in your life to perform what it was sent to do.

May the word of the Lord run swiftly and be glorified in you.

—2 Thessalonians 3:1

Chapter One
INFORMATION OVERLOAD

The Dance of Two Camps.

—Song of Solomon 6:13

It would seem that early in my life I was always pulled in the direction of my senses. The fragrance of a flower coming into bloom and blowing on the breeze, the smell of fresh bread or cookies baking in the oven, the feeling of my sheets fresh from the clothesline with their crisp fragrance and touch, the sight of the sun glistening on a wet leaf in the morning light, the taste of marmalade's tang on a crusty piece of toast in the morning…the whole of my life, I have been sensory-oriented. I have found that most people are information oriented. They may look at the very same things as I do, but they look to discover something they feel is important to *know*. I experience everything intrinsically for the experience itself and all the hidden insights available about God within it. This has been a problem for me most of my life. Now, I consider it to be a matter of design.

We were designed for the invisible life of the spirit realm and the experience of it. Human beings were created by God to know and understand how the hidden spirit realm interacts with the visible natural one that seems so much more real to us. I have often felt like my lens finder has been installed backwards because this hidden world seems so real to me! As a child raised with a name like "Faith," I have found it too easy to find a storyline invisible to others - to believe in things hidden from view, at times. This has been a blessing in my life but was often viewed as my downfall and due to my immaturity, I believed I myself was flawed. My childlike wonder of the invisible realm was designed to believe God, and so it was in this area that I inevitably suffered the greatest wounds. And those wounds created a filter that spoke, "unloved, ugly, childish, stupid, useless" so that I could not receive love even when it was offered in sincerity to me.

In childhood it was challenging to find context for this unique internal design. It didn't get any easier until I was in my 30's. At 32, in the midst of deep brokenness, I dedicated my life to being a Christian, or a "Christ-follower." That was how this new way of life was introduced to me. In short, you dedicate your life to God, accepting the sacrifice that Jesus made by becoming the eternal price for the sins of all mankind through his sacrificial death on the cross. Our Father raised him from the grave three days later in the greatest display of power to that point in human history. Jesus had delivered his own blood as an offering to his Father for all the horrible separation of sin. By his sacrifice, he destroyed sin's power once and for all in that moment.

Jesus then took a seat next to his Father, put his feet up and said, "Let the fun begin. My sisters and brothers are going to kick some devil butt and we are going to watch the show!" I was taught he gave me a set of keys. With these keys I was able to lock up the enemy and unlock the shackles of those the enemy had bound. I even received a fresh inundation of the Spirit-led life through the baptism of the Holy Spirit which gave me a language, power, gifts and skills to help me beat our enemy. What a grand story, don't you agree? I know I am speaking lightly of deep truths, but I saw it as a story that I was not so much a participant in, but that had been written for me to discover my part. In my pursuit to find my own place in that storyline, I would often dig deeper than most.

It was there that I discovered a realm that, though invisible to most, could be interacted with on a daily basis. Everything began to change for me as I embraced that discovery and the adventure. Even more astonishing, I discovered that God was not a being in the sky watching me with a gavel, ready to smash me like an ant under his judgement. He was a loving father. He had a son, Jesus, who was my big brother (Rom. 8:29)! Together they had pulled off the heist of all eternity - stealing back the hearts of their family through a radical sacrifice against which their enemy could never win. Even more compelling to me was the fact that God had a spirit and because I was created in his exact image, so did I. His spirit and mine co-exist in a realm that though invisible, was more real than the visible realm I could see around me.

I want to honor the men and women of God that I followed so diligently. They taught me to revere the Word of

God - the Holy Bible. I was taught to pray, correctly. I was given opportunities to serve others, with excellence. I was gifted with the belief that only excellence pleases God because he is perfect. And that I would never be truly excellent until I saw him physically one day at the great throne where he sits with his Father, awaiting an evaluation of my life. And I learned that I could continue to work towards it on the Earth and would be rewarded for that at the end of my life when I died. However, I wondered how much of the rewards he meant for me to have would be left undiscovered, because I never seemed to reach that standard of excellence that was lifted before me. It was truly in my heart to please God and that standard seemed clearly visible to those around me. Religious works of service, faithfulness, and humility had become the standard for excellence.

I dedicated 15 years of my life to trying to figure out that formula for successful Christian living and fulfill it. Yet it was challenging for me to see that I was surrounded by the defeat, depression, and death in church culture – and in my own life, too. To a girl who was desperately seeking for love and acceptance, this way of life was always hard. I subconsciously knew that something was missing or perhaps had been left out of the story. My search was more often focused on being loved, than on doing the right thing. I tried to do the right thing so it wouldn't be so hard to love me. Inevitably I was setup to fail.

We cannot earn what has already been freely given.

God doesn't want us to know His open hand before we experience His joyful heart of exuberance! But I was so broken by family – natural and spiritual – that I could not accept His love and affirmation. There was a truth I could not see while blinded by all the experiences I had been exposed to in my broken family dynamics. A part of me was always looking for family and I falsely believed the search was in me because I had been cruelly gifted with such a broken one.

At the age of 16, I ran away from home and that family. Within a few months of leaving, I was pregnant. By 18 I was married to a man who felt trapped and had two children. I was depressed, a high school dropout, and in the depths of poverty. Eventually my husband found a better life that didn't include me. Once again, I felt unloved and rejected. I fought for custody of my daughter and son. They were the only family I felt I could trust. My parents and siblings had all moved to the south by then, leaving me in the New York alone. I spent years trying to build a family for my children and I, going from one broken abusive relationship to another. My search for a good family on the Earth to make me whole again failed me over and over. Layers of hurt and frustration seemed to cement the idea that there was something deeply wrong with me. Yet, in coming into relationship with God and reading his promises in the Bible, I sensed I was made for so much more.

I have had to come to the realization that my truth, my "fit" could not be realized by accessing the idea that human relationship alone was meant to fulfill me. No, I had to look beyond those painful experiences I had in relationship, and beyond even humanity's story. I found the story of the ages buried like golden treasure in the Word of God!

God loves the Earth, and he loves humanity. He created us for family! He is our family, and we are his! The Kingdom of God is not a serfdom with castles and lords full of masters to please and service to perform. It is a family affair of the grandest dimensions. It encompasses all of creation by wrapping us into divinity through a restorative relationship and deep transformational experiences with the presence and power of God. This relationship with God is not enough! It is through knowing his written word and doing life with those in his family that healing and wholeness come. Faith in God alone is not enough. Faith finds its expression through love and the love we long for is in us to cause us to know God as a Father, Jesus as our big brother, and in experience the incredible family dynamic called the Body of Christ.

We are part of a family that is spread across time and exceeds physical locations. This mystery reveals to us the true beauty of the nature of God's spirit and the invisible realm out of which this visible realm exists. We are called to an adventure in an invisible world that interacts with and overtakes this natural realm. That realm and its realities are meant to be the source of our story and out of which we experience fatherhood and family. The identity we have there gives us the power to change here. Nothing in our human story can withstand the love and power of that truth.

In one of the hardest seasons of my life, I dove into God's Word with deep hunger and spent much time alone with Him. It was at that time that I met a company of people who welcomed me as family and began to study the Bible with me around tables meant for discussion. We literally ate the word of God together as our primary meal; although there were often other delectable treats at that table that we shared! It around that table with those people that I gained the perspective that family is the answer to all types of divides. With that discovery, my true adventure began, and that is what I want to share with you in this book. That discovery wrecked my theology. It caused me to examine my belief in God, myself, and the Church. I was deconstructing but not to like Humpty-Dumpty who could not be put back together again. No, this in-authentic identity and flawed framework for family gave way to a new way of life full of adventures and relationships all over the world! I have discovered I truly have family in every nation on the globe and some of them are meant to be interacted with in close and intimate relationship despite our incredible physical distance from each other.

My Christian life has been full of information from great men and women of God. I was blessed to be born in a time when media allowed me to access information at a level that honestly was as exciting for me as it was overwhelming. I learned about the truths of scriptures from others. I even became so adept in my learning that I was chosen to teach and lead others in what I learned. I have notebooks, electronic files, and memories of all the best doctrines of the charismatic and evangelical denominations, all held in tension within a "non-denominational" movement that seemed to be a denomination of its own. I was proud of my learning and yet secretly, often confused by it.

You see, my experiences with Father God and Jesus that were sensory-oriented (as I was), could never quite seem to perfectly align with the doctrine of those around me. Even more confusing is the fact that though I was adept at teaching and preaching those doctrines, I was more often sought out for the "experiences" I could afford people in the place we call "prayer," where God would speak to me and through me.

I could touch Him amid an audience yearning for him and do so in such a way that they too would be engaged in their senses – their soul and mind with him. I facilitated that experience as often as I was allowed. It was my favorite place to be. I was told by a dear mentor that my greatest skill was to cause a person or group of people, whether 1 or 500, to feel like they were sitting across the table from God having a cup of coffee with him. I was there in the room, but he was who they heard and experienced. For me, those were the moments when my life just made sense. I would shed this feeling of being a square peg being forced to fit into a round hole, and just sink into this powerful knowing that this is what I was designed for - knowing HIM! Yet, though I would experience this in my personal life often, it was like a wave of the ocean that came and then was pulled out again by the tide. The rhythms of the doctrines around me and the movements of all the sharp edges of the broken people serving with me in this grand Christian life would exert such pressure on me. It would take from me the joy of those intimate experiences with him, like the ocean pulling away the tide. I would feel guilty for letting him slip away from me. I identified with the woman in Song of Solomon 6:12-13 who lived with a heart divided, pulled by two worlds.

Shulamite: Before I was even aware, my soul had made me as the chariots of my noble people.

Beloved and His friends: Return, return, O Shulamite; return, return, that we may look upon you!

Shulamite: What would you see in the Shulamite - as it were, the dance of two camps?

Song of Solomon is a love story about a woman and her lover. It is also a wonderful analogy of the relationship between God and his people. We are the woman and God is the lover. This woman had been on a journey of learning to trust the ways of her lover. Yet, she has an experience where she was compelled by her friends' voices of need to come and be with them. She left the garden place - the relational proximity to her lover in order to go a distance away to be with them. She hears his voice calling to her and realized she didn't even notice the lack of proximity to him until that moment. Her companions' voices were so compelling that she didn't miss her feet leaving that garden space with him. She cries out, realizing that she had a divided soul life – *the dance of two camps* - a foot in both places of relationship. Rather than invite her friends into that garden space of relationship, she left it to be with them.

Isn't that something we are all guilty of at times? How many times a day do you leave God behind in terms of personal heart preference to pursue or be present for others? I had a very divided lifestyle, and it was literally mentally and emotionally breaking me down. My desire to be seen and known by God's people so that I could feel love would call me to grand acts of service that frankly called to me like the Shulamite's companions called to her. I was capable physically of doing them, but spiritually I would leave God's pleasure and delight to be a servant to the many. Until I found myself dry, dusty, and desperate and listening for his voice even as I cried out to him. I lived that life of service to others for God and yet somehow it meant I had to leave him as a personal heart preference, my first place, to do everything that others needed me to be for them. I considered these acts of service a matter of duty to him, but never paid attention to how they left me empty inside.

My life was an orchestration of moments spent with God that were compelling and then living out of them as an overflow until I was dry, dusty, and desperate. I would escape into him and find that joy of his presence. Filling myself up, I would go pour out to others and then return to him after. One of the greatest evidences of the power of his love is that even in the erratic rhythm of living in this back and forth, I still became more and more like him. Each time I hosted his presence for others, I would myself be compelled! I found healing and restoration in those moments of visitation. My confidence in him was growing and my prophetic gifting grew legs and took off running so that sometimes even *I* had to keep up with it! I thought this was just what Christian living was about. I wished for a constant steady experience of togetherness with God but the cares of this world, the responsibility I took from others, the sickness in my own body and the doctrines of men together created that sucking pressure of the tide pulling the experiences from me into the abyss of demand around me. But I wanted more. I wanted to be more.

There is a heart space that God wants all of us to embrace. In Luke 8:10, Mark 4:25, Proverbs 9:9, 12:1 and 2 Timothy 2:2 we are encouraged to remain teachable. To always be open to having the ability to learn something new, even if that destroys the foundation of something we were once told was true. **Any fact that is not founded in truth will have to submit to God's love and his amazing passion for you and your design, soon or later.** Although I was blessed to have access to so much knowledge about God, the knowledge itself needed to submit to God's love and his own ability to teach me and correct me, himself. My seemingly backwards lens that allowed me to gaze experientially into truth with a desire to truly know God in a deep and abiding way, had submitted to the desires of men to instruct me, disciple me, and gain my support of their mission. I so longed for affirmation from men that I lost the childlike wonder of having my heavenly father approve of me in favor of the more tangible and public affirmation of men. In doing so, lost the tangible sense of God's presence and purpose, for me as an experience.

I took on these good things about submitting to the leadership of men but with the motive of gaining their affirmation. I settled into a way of life where I was believing with everyone else what I was told to believe. I elevated intelligence in such a way that I felt the need to intellectualize every single experience I had with God. Though scripture clearly tells us that God's ways are so much higher and different than our ways (Isaiah 55:8-9), I had fallen prey to needing to explain everything I knew about God to men, and this was my downfall. I am smart enough to understand much of what God was showing me, but often what I experienced was not easily explained to the scholars around me. I became adept at doing what the Bible says in Matthew 7:6 – casting the wisdom of God I had been gifted with before those who had no appreciation for the deeper truths God was sharing with me. They had already decided what to believe and did not appreciate that I might think differently or have experienced something different.

There are truths that God will reveal to you that are meant to be treasure for adornment, tools for victory, or wisdom for gaining understanding that takes us deeper on a quest into God's heart. Your personal quest to know God and the experiences you have with him should always be confirmed with the word of God, but it doesn't always merit sharing or explaining to others. In 1 Corinthians 4:1, Paul describes himself as a steward of the mysteries of God. Some things are meant to be stewarded by being tucked away until you have so integrated them into your understanding that they are a part of who you are now. They are no longer mysteries but that which you know as truth and have become yourself.

I was gifted in the supernatural, in healing, prayer, and even as a teacher. The more I developed these areas of my life, the more it required me to compartmentalize my Christian life. The areas that were valuable to others weren't congruent in comparison to other areas that I was struggling personally with. I learned to put those struggles away and hide them on a back shelf while I allowed the other more appealing attributes to shine at the front. If it was valuable to someone else, especially spiritually valuable, I let it be seen. But if it was a character struggle, a matter of doubt or shame, I hid it in a carefully constructed box with a label only I could see. I grew spiritually while other areas of my soul and mind lay dormant, hidden away and unchallenged by light.

Hiding in the dark when God is telling you to trust him in the light is hard! It requires you to organize lies, storylines, secrets into compartments in your soul and mind. Compartmentalization is a difficult thing to manage! It left cracks for sin to come and hide out in my life. If you believe the darkness can be controlled, you will fall prey to hiding what you think you can control from being seen or influencing you. We are children of the light and not meant to hide darkness inside. In my Christian life I had more questions than answers sometimes, based often on the condition of my own soul. Those questions often came down to the "whys" of the Christian faith life. How could so much sin, decay and disease be present amongst us?

How could we be so powerless in our humanity if God gave us so much power in Jesus? I prayed for a young woman to live and not die after she overdosed on drugs and lay in a hospital bed dying, but she didn't live. Why?

More so, how could we be so Christian but so without compassion and love in our everyday life? Christians often used me to get closer to my leaders or treated me carelessly as if I had no value but to serve their own needs. I would hide myself in the secret place of the Most High as Psalm 91 declares we can and should. But I would come out of it and face a harsh reality. Even God's people can be mean. Agendas that serve God are often a mixture of man and God. If you don't agree or if you tend to ask too many questions, you might be accused of pride. Worse, you might be treated like a dumb student. One who has not truly encountered truth and therefore needs to be sat down and taught again.

This culture served to elevate the search for intelligent knowledge of the ways of God and his holy scriptures. How could I come to terms with the dichotomy of this faith culture that I was living in and pursuing God within? "Truth versus experience" became synonymous with right versus wrong rather than complementary.

The place of the spirit realm and the supernatural became my own secret fascination. I have had incredible encounters with Jesus and Father God. But I lived my Christian faith out in a culture that was more comfortable talking about the Bible, then its author. I would be pulled out for special moments when people wanted to hear from God, like an antenna adjusted on a television set or on the roof of a house. And then I would be put back in my place and given the opportunity to parrot the knowledge of others who entrusted me to say it the way they would. In one moment, it was exhilarating to take others into the throne room of God to hear His voice and feel His love. And in other moments, I felt like an exchange student that had been privileged to go to school in America at an amazing university but had no true family around them who wanted to get to know them and help them grow. My leaders were oriented towards grooming me for a function, as you groom an athlete to achieve a trophy in their hand and be placed upon a platform. But I was just a girl who was searching for a family and unconditional love.

To discover God's heart beyond the rigid doctrines I was living within, I had to encounter the unconditional love of a father, from God Himself. He was faithful to put a man of God in my life with the DNA of a spiritual father and set me within a family of faith full of flaws growing together in grace. Interestingly, we met at a fellowship for leaders outside of denominational lines or competitive frameworks that churches can fall into. I met him at dinner table at an invitation from a couple who understand hospitality and the joy this setting can spark for faith and fellowship. This meeting unraveled many layers of my life when it happened. Yet looking back now, I feel like I was just like a fat woman who had squeezed herself into a tight girdle to appear more appealing but now has escaped its confining restraint. Having experienced trying to look a certain way through the tight confines of spandex, I can tell you it is not comfortable to wear, and it is oh so liberating to release yourself from them. For me, taking off the spandex girdle was to be done in the privacy of my home, where others could not see what spilled out. I never imagined that there was a way of life where my spillage and my beauty might become all together a beautiful thing meant to be seen?! To be naked, authentic, transparent, and truthful and feel seen, known and loved? Could that be possible in this life?

It is possible for every believer in God's Kingdom family! My freedom to be God's child the way that he designed me came at a great personal cost, but I have no regrets! Trying to find context for my freedom in the lives of others not only bound me tightly but crimped my own personal style! I demonstrated a ridiculous inability to perfectly fit any mold, and it tore my soul over and over. And when it did, the pain I had hidden there often leaked out like a leaky water spigot that I couldn't shut off. It flooded my life and the life of others around me. It cost me spiritually, emotionally, and physically. My hope is that as you read my story and the blessed discoveries that God helped me to make along the way, you might feel seen, known and loved in the same way. May you be released into authentic relationship with God, yourself and others!

I saw a book cover by Maya Angelou recently titled, "When the Caged Bird Sings." I thought inside of me, "I wonder what happens when the caged bird is no longer caged…and she still sings!?" This book is me singing! I have been set free into the glorious liberty of true freedom to be me, according to original design. Into an imperfect but authentic relationship with God, my designer. There are laws governing the outcomes of many things around us. Science and physics demonstrate this to us all the time. Even mathematics in its most rudimentary forms give us expected outcomes. The only liberty we have that will change those outcomes is through our freedom of choice. I am free to choose God. And so are you. I choose the liberty of life. I pray you hear the heart of this book and experience this glorious freedom, too! I pray that the song of freedom I am singing here captivates you, drawing you out of the doctrines of men and demons and into the liberty and lightness of the Kingdom of God. May you find hope for loving family again. May you discover the God of creation and His handiwork in and through His family called the Body of Christ, on the Earth today and throughout the ages to come!

Life Application

1. In this chapter the author describes how vital her way of seeing and experiencing the world was to her. How do you see and experience the world? What senses and measurements are involved?

2. There is very compelling aspect to religion that can frame the way you think about yourself and others. How have you "learned" to identify God, leaders, other people? Who taught you to do that?

3. Have you ever shared something and then regretted it later? What has God spoken to you that you carelessly shared, maybe in excitement or for confirmation and affirmation from others?

4. What have you learned to be, that doesn't really fit you...describe your girdle!

5. Take a moment and ask God to help you strip that off. Write down in your journal what freedom from that feels like and looks like.

Chapter Two
SUBSIDIZING INTIMACY

Hope left undiscovered will not mold. It will simply expire.

—**Faith Allison**

I don't want you to think that I have regrets about the years of visiting God and then hosting his presence for others. The spaces that I formerly spent self-comforting and avoiding pain have all been overtaken by joy! The journey to embracing that joy is mine to walk, even as Jesus embraced the pain of the journey to the cross. Hebrews 12:2 declares that Jesus endured the pain and the shame of the cross to gain the joy that was set before him as he sat down at the right hand of the Father in his family position. I never want to be an advocate of intentional pain, but what I am suggesting is that God is not only the author of our life story, but its finisher too. The pen that he has written my story in has been dipped in the blood of Jesus Christ, the first pure and sinless man who took on sin so his blood would speak forever against it. That blood speaks not just the sweet blessings of my life, but also forensically of every avenue of escape, restoration, and recompense. Because of the power of the creativity of our designer to take what seems like loss and death and turn it into life and joy again, there is a joy available to all of us, just as it was to Jesus.

Life continues to present us with challenges every year we are alive. My most recent life challenge was a big one. It was relational, painful, shocking and I felt it try to rend my soul. But it could not! Instead, I found that though my mind was not adequately prepared, my spirit was! I found a well-spring of joy and new levels of freedom even as I surrendered to the grief and loss that came with releasing that old life. I felt like Jesus was standing right next to me saying, "We are going to get through this. Keep walking with me. No! Don't stop and look at that. Don't take the bait. Embrace freedom without shame. This is going to be so much better, and we (Jesus and Poppa God) are going to keep you engaged and alive and thriving during what would buckle the knees of others."

This truly was the first time I did not go back to being alone in comforting myself, or folding inward to escape from the circumstances I found myself in. I was not numb. I was alive and grateful. I found myself able to not fixate on what had occurred. There was a grace to not look back and try to understand it all, and I embraced it wholeheartedly. How did this happen? It began with getting understanding.

Gaining sound judgment is key, so first things first: go after Lady Wisdom! Now, whatever else you do, follow through to understanding. Cherish her, and she will help you rise above the confusion of life. Your possibilities will open up before you. Embrace her, and she will raise you to a place of honor in return. She will provide the finishing touch to your character—grace; she will give you an elegant confidence.

—Proverbs 4:5-9 (VOICE)

This passage speaks of knowledge, or sound judgment (as this translation refers to it) then wisdom, and lastly, understanding. I had spent my life pursuing knowledge, because the world values knowledge tremendously. I had gained wisdom from the great men and women of God positioned in my path. But understanding had escaped me. I *did* not *value the pursuit of it* because I was too busy subsidizing the intimate spaces of my life to other lesser lovers.

In my early years of life, when I was too young to understand what was happening to me, I was violently introduced to false intimacy. I was sexually molested at a very young age. It opened a door in my life that kind of just swung on its hinges in the wind of life. Once opened, it let in whatever and whomever thought they had a right to me. The doors of my heart and mind were like swinging saloon doors rather than a bedroom door with a lock from the inside. The violation of my intimate spaces –physically, mentally, and spiritually – by someone who was meant to be trusted created a deep fear of crisis in me. It also caused me to lose the natural capacity children have, to expect unconditional love. I grew up instead, expecting my voice to be silenced, walls to be pushed through and pain to come. I accepted the lie that I was not lovable. I did not feel safe, loved or as if there was a place in the world that I belonged to. I could never explain this to myself or to another person adequately in a way that could change that cycle. I falsely believed that it needed to be proved wrong and my own value affirmed to change the outcomes of that cycle. It created a lot of fear and confusion in my life.

It also allowed me to be victimized again and again. I was raped twice as an adult woman. I remember that both times I was raped, I did not fight back. I didn't even report it. I just waited for it to end and even wondered in my mind's escape if I must die for it to end. In my thoughts, clear as a bell while I was violently being raped the second time, "You must be really broken to not be fighting against this and choosing to think about death instead." I was very deeply broken inside. Those swinging saloon doors let in whatever life told me I had to let in. Forcibly, unwillingly, and even coaxingly, I let the private spaces of my heart, soul and body be used by others. This formed a very deeply distorted viewpoint of intimacy in my mind.

Sexual abuse is a deliberate choice by one person to weaponize their body against another person. In that moment not only are they violating someone personally, but they are opening a spiritual portal for evil to begin a powerful dialogue with their victim about their value and self-worth full of lies. That evil process leads to all kinds of false beliefs, behaviors, and decisions that in turn further false intimacy within themselves and with others. The enemy of our soul despises our ability to know God intimately and will do anything to disrupt that true and honest place in our heart and mind. Those belief systems he implants are like unholy fertilizer in a dark garden bearing dark beliefs like weeds, by which we suffer consequences that have nothing to do with our true identity.

God does not make mistakes! Nor does he create anything without a capacity for it to be subdued or to subdue another. Until we recover that fractured territory of our soul, mind, and body we cannot hope to escape those actions based on those lies. No defense we build can withstand the onslaught of enemies when the door of our soul is open to them in places we refuse to visit personally and let God into. We cannot subdue the voices permanently, nor keep those trespassing, often violent spirits, out of our circle of control without God's help. With compassionate community and in relationship with him we can become healed and whole. At our core, we were all made by God to be intimate with God. First with Him and then if we are so blessed, with a loving spouse. Children and close friendships with others who form a sense of tribe or belonging fill in that space with such a joyful challenge that we are strengthened in our spirit, fattened in our souls and kept healthy in our bodies. No one can or should live outside of close, connected community. We are not meant to be alone. God made it impossible for us to be satisfied with him alone. He wants the overflow from our deep knowledge of him to have somewhere to go. He is indeed a God of unreasonable abundance!

Over the years I have made many bad decisions in order to be loved. Even after surrendering my heart and life to the Lord, I still struggled with carelessly giving away my life to others. Though committed to valuing my life in God, I continued to struggle to keep out trespassers, hurtful habits and people who often took his place. I had to do a deep work on my soul to discover why my boundaries were so easily crossed or given over to the worship of others. It was then that I realized how deeply the sexual assault had impacted me. It was determined to steal my identity from me by misplacing my affections in a perverse way. My body and soul would send me all kinds of warnings about misusing them, but I was adept at ignoring the obvious and unable to see the truth about what was happening in my relationships. I would often find myself overlooking the obvious cues that I was tired, in favor of stretching my life to help others. I fed off of the idea that Christian service is the art of giving your life away for God.

In Skye Jethani's book, "With: Reimagining the Way You Relate To God,"[1] he describes five typical postures of relationship with God: Life For God, Life Under God, Life Over God and Life From God. The one that I was so familiar with was living my life for God as a servant trying to gain affirmation, serving him in great acts of sacrifice. Sounds so Christian, right? To make matters more difficult to navigate, I was surrounded by people in a faith movement with the "Life Over God" perspective. I had many leaders with prophetic voices who were incredibly gifted at hearing God's voice but would often submit what they heard to business and organizational formulas with controllable outcomes. Everything was built upon a person's capacity to lead and the capacity of others to serve them on mission. I often observed very little personal ownership of the mission God had given a man, in others. Yet I was regularly encouraged to sacrifice my own mission for the mission of others. It was a recipe for rapid growth, but the people around me were often a mile wide and a foot deep in their own spirituality. Often, they would be wandering in their hearts as they served a dream one person received from God while pondering what to do with their own dream from God.

I have also observed what Skye described as "Life From God" which is focused on consumerism. It is to want God's blessings more than you want him. To use God to get our desires met and forsake the giver himself in the process is such a perversion of relationship for the Christian life. Yet many churches are full of this type of relationship today. Many of our budgets for outreach or finances for discipleship are built upon the value of wealth stemming from this imperfect bedrock. When pain or disappointment or cultural shifts threaten this value system for success over God, the foundations of ministry built on this often splinter, lose their stability, and fail to grow because its bedrock is built on people gaining wealth or abundance and a portion of it being transferred to that ministry on a scheduled predictive cycle. The God of the universe who owns everything everywhere, who provides for his children and the missions he gives to them, has been replaced with the fallacies and abilities of man to be obedient to support the vision of the local church. It is a hard place to find yourself in. Obedience out of working to please God is a tough place to find yourself in.

Obedience flows out of a heart space of love and relationship that appreciates the fact that everything you have comes from God and he wants to give you so much more!

Teaching people to love God should never replace demonstrating how he loves connected community that responds to the condition of the lives of those within. It is a beautiful thing to find a tribe of people who demonstrate and discuss openly the love of the Father!

It took personal relationship with God, deep places of introspection in the secret place of His heart, and spirit-led counselors to help me realign spirit, soul and body in Him, first and foremost. In times of prayer contending for my own soul to be free from the past that tried to claim it, I allowed the power of the Word of God to cleanse my soul (my mind, will and emotions) daily to be free. This evil tendency to self-harm by allowing anyone and anything to steal from me did not leave easily. To not honor yourself the way God sees you or to not expect others to see your value is false humility and a lie. We don't have value because someone told us we do. We are valued because our Father is God and we are His children. God does not make crap. Nor does He make you valuable only after you have jumped through ten hoops to prove your worth.

Every single person in God's family is significant no matter their age, gender, race, or ethnic background. From the start of our life, we all have a very deliberate purpose in God and the entire Earth is waiting for you to step into that immediately! No matter how imperfectly you do it, if this is your goal and your passion, you have permission to from God himself! Even as you try and fail, he will not turn his back on you or cut you out of his life because of your learning curve. This was another pattern of self-harm in my life that had to be defeated. God's peace and wholeness in my life were stifled under great acts of service for others, or as I thought of it - "for God." I worked harder than most to make sure everyone else was setup for success. When others gave me negative feedback or criticized me, I would regularly allow their words to be like death over my body as I experienced the pain and rejection of this cycle. I expected fatigue as a constant companion. I pushed down the voice that cried out for escape. I silenced the bubbly essence of joy trying to find its way out of my spirit. I was a harsh task master for my body, mind, and soul. I had been trained well in that by my natural father.

Our family was known for our work ethic. We were taught to ignore pain; work hard and only celebrate when you were done. I don't really remember much celebrating! Neglect is a form of abuse. We see this in the court systems with parental neglect of children. It carries a harsh punishment. But God's children are often trained in this system long before they entered a church. They follow this same pattern in ministry and call it holiness and compassion for others. We exchange the light and easy yoke that God promises us for a life of service that often holds more weight with our soul than our own well-being or that of our family's well-being. This is the voice of the old covenant law and religion speaking. This is not the way of the children of God, as new covenant sons and daughters. Our "doings" are meant to come out of our "being" with

God on a journey with others. If you are unfamiliar with the difference, keep reading. I will go into depth on this later in the story.

I have found that many forms of faith have developed a set of beliefs that encourage them to neglect the care of their own soul. Yet without a healthy soul, our spirit becomes stymied, our body gets sick, and our calling or purpose finds itself under siege by our enemy. 3 John 1:2 promises us a prosperity that is directly linked to the health of our soul. ***Our soul is meant to be the clear lens between the physical body and the spirit of a man.*** In life it gets marred, fractured and deeply stained by sin - ours and others. Is there any wonder that we are unable to do what we desire to in our spirit? Or break free of the sinful patterns that our body and mind are so willing to follow?

The power of a clear soul aligned with a strong spirit will subdue a physical body so that it willingly follows suit. To have your body respond to your spirit not as an act of submission, but as a willing assent to the adventure ahead that *love* has formed for the child of God is the greatest gift you can find in this life. Imagine all of you being engaged with joy and strength no matter how hard something is? We rarely find this place of engagement. At least that has been my experience.

John 10:10 declares that our enemy is a thief who comes to steal, kill, and destroy us. I remember wondering if God had a bad day communicating with John the author of that text when he wrote it. How can you destroy something you have already killed? Later through an encounter with the Lord I came to accept that what the enemy is intent on stealing from us is our capacity for faith! You see faith only works through the agent of love. Like bread void of baking soda, we fall flat of our full capacity. If you don't know you are loved, your faith life will be small and caged. It will be void of power even if you attend church faithfully and read the Bible daily. Without the revelation of love, you will do no great things with your faith-life for the Kingdom of God. I have also seen a perversion of this where people who love themselves more than God can use the power of faith to obtain cars, houses, bank accounts and grand experiences in life, all for themselves under the guise of pleasing God.

The faith life described in Hebrews 11 and 12 is not about self-adornment. It is a league of legacy builders who surrendered their own lives as part of a storyline greater than their own! They are not listing what they gained in this passage, but who they became, what that meant to God and to us who came after them. Noah was an ark builder in a time when arks were unheard of. Enoch walked with God more than most men until God's house became closer to him than his own, and he failed to come home to the Earth again. Abraham and Sarah followed God when he told them to pack and go to a new place – but didn't tell them the location! Can you imagine? In our GPS-rich society, we refuse to go anywhere we can't find our own way too! Even Sarah's laugh of "how," regarding her pending pregnancy didn't keep her faith from being mentioned in this chapter. So many others are listed there too.

Their un-normal calling was the entry fee to this hall of heroes listed as God's favorites. It is the hall of the heroes of faith who sacrificed, surrendered, and even died without obtaining what they had stood in faith for that are championed here like works of art in a gallery for us. Their lives displayed, flaws and all so that we ourselves could understand that we can obtain life without any work at all because Jesus truly finished it all! We inherit their legacy and their reward! More importantly, we inherit His!

Here is the truth captured in John 10:10. If the enemy of our soul can steal our faith by convincing our minds and bodies that we are unlovable or unworthy of being loved than he has easy access to killing our calling and destiny. He wants to kill the purpose of God that you represent on the Earth! Without purpose, we are left to destruction. Like the rest of the world, we are like blind sheep without a purpose other than to blindly follow what everyone else is doing. We follow the herd and forsake Him in us. Proverbs 29:18 declares that without vision we are merely perishing and are like sheep being led to slaughter (Acts 8:32). Hopelessness sets in and hope deferred, or never realized, leads to disease and death. (Proverbs 13:12) The entire world is collectively being led into death by this cycle. Many Christians have joined this movement towards mindless, hopeless, and purposeless death, their callings left undiscovered or fulfilled.

I had to do the hard work of cleaning out the closet of my soul, making room for joy to arise and take up space by cooperating with the easy grace of forgiveness. I began reframing the way I thought about myself according to my identity as a child of God. I pushed back any and all thoughts – even those of others – that did not come from a loving place or a truthful tone. I couldn't do that until I knew what God said about me. This came with a revelation again. We will talk about that in the next chapter. For now, I want to ask you this question.

Have you farmed out the favor of God on your life by subsidizing the intimacy meant only for him to others? Is he your first thought and last thought each day? Because that is what love does. Or does he share you with a multitude of other loves and hobbies? He wants to be your everything. I promise you that he will satisfy you more than any of those other lovers could ever hope to satisfy. And it's a satisfaction that grows deeper and deeper day by day. Enoch in the Bible was so satisfied by God's love that he forgot to come back to Earth! I want to be that way with God. Don't you? What could these saints of old have discovered that was so enticing that they could follow God into the unknown so freely?

I believe a driving passion for God is meant to sustain us, as well as reframe our life so that everything in us and around us submits to the personal preference for God that this lifestyle fosters. Without Him we are hopelessly trying to better ourselves, like a homeowner trying to operate appliances without a startup manual. We can all learn and grow through use. But our blind miscalculations can create stress on our design, wear on our soul and often cause us to measure the wrong things. **Are you living like a solution, or a statistic?** Is there a driving purpose to your life that stems from the heart of God and his design for you or are you living by default in your Christian life, led by the instructions and demonstrations of others around you? Have you talked to your architect and read the manual for yourself? You should. It's the best starting place for discovering who he is.

Life Application

1. How have you subsidized the intimate spaces of your heart and life to other lovers?

2. Are there territories in your soul that have been fractured? In what way?

3. How might these fractures be affecting your ability to be intimate with God? With others?

4. What closets in your soul need to be cleaned out?

5. What truth in this chapter gives you faith to see yourself as a solution rather than a statistic?

Chapter Three
ARRESTED BY HIS FRAGRANCE

He is altogether lovely. This is my beloved and this is my friend.

—Song of Solomon 5:16

I have to tell you that there is a place close to God's heart that is so tangible that at times I have put my physical hand out to touch him, expecting to feel the fabric on his chest. I have slapped the knee of Jesus as he sat next to me and expected my hand to contact his leg as we laughed together! Yet, those moments were not as often as I would have liked. And I was taught that this was not to be pursued. That the only true substance of him that could be trusted was his holy scriptures - the Bible. I love my Bible. If you could see how dog eared and worn out it is, you would laugh and ask me to get a new one. I have several other translations and love to spread them out across my table to study. I have access to the biblical library online via the internet. I have read more books, studied more articles, and written more notes than Sunday dinners I've eaten in my entire life to this point. I love to read and study!

When I was a child, my father would take us to the library every Saturday. I would fill a bag with as many books as I could cram into it and then carry it home as a treasure chest to be hoarded. I vicariously lived through those books! My childhood was very difficult with many traumas and wounds that would take me years to recover from. Yet, those books and that love of learning could never be taken from me. At times when my father would ground me and take the physical books away from me for weeks at a time, I would sit in my room behind a closed door, locked out from the benefits of family and relationship. My books were taken away, but I would sit waiting for it to be over and reinvent the world around me as an escape of sorts. The window of my bedroom faced the street in front of our home. It became a portal to the storyline of others like in one of my precious books. I would sit watching the traffic and people walking or riding bikes by our home. I allowed my imagination to discover what they were saying, filling in narratives that would have made you chuckle! I am a storyteller at heart. I was made for stories. Even in the absence of a visit to the library, the liberties of childhood, or the physical presence of a book in my hand, I could tell a story and read it to myself with such vivid detail you would have thought I was reading from a script! I taught my granddaughter to do this before she even was able to read herself. She too has a vivid imagination! Watching her sit in her car seat telling me stories about the moon in the sky and how it was playing peek-a-boo with her as she saw it disappear and reappear amongst the rooftops from the car window as we drove home, made for amazing stories to be retold to others about her creativity later on.

We were made to be story tellers and to find our place in a story that is so much grander than ourselves. It demands community and forces a desire for belonging. Alone, I can do small things. Together, I can do so much more. I wonder often if my love of studying was really just a hunger for adventures with God, and the longing to share that experiential hunger with you.

After a particularly painful betrayal, I found myself in the familiar place of nestling into God defensively. In my work today as a trauma therapist today, I call this the art of "folding." You may be familiar with the responses to crisis which are normal - fight or flight. In trauma work, we find three other responses - flooding, freezing and folding. Flooding is to have your entire being washed through with so much emotion that you can't control it at all. Freezing is to pause like a deer in headlights and not be able to give an appropriate or expected response. Folding is the response of withdrawal with extreme measures. It is to pull internally into a space that is safe and dark and comforting. When it is developed as a habitual response to your former trauma experiences being triggered in the present, you can even develop a disorder that prevents you from leaving your own home to escape being triggered again! It is so powerful in its pull towards safety. It will cause you to back away from things you should not. It will allow you to crumble in adversity and internalize the responsibility for the events around you.

My way of dealing with crisis was folding, by grounding myself emotionally and physically, just like my father used to as a punishment when I was a child. I would shut myself in a room with God to find him in the comfort of the silence and if I could not find him there easily, I would think it was my fault. My sin had separated him from me. There I would surrender to the old comforts that served me in the past - eating, sleeping, watching TV, reading novels. Waiting…waiting…for that grounding season to end. Falsely believing that someone would let me out when I had paid that debt of time off.

The only difference in this season of life was that I had discovered God was always there with me in that space. I would alternate back and forth between relenting to the guilt of what had happened, with talking with him about what had happened, just trying to figure it out. It would consume my conversation with him and if I didn't get an answer quickly than I would allow my inner child to feel punished and relent to the pull of the old comforts. It is a vicious and awful cycle. If you are caught in it yourself, I want you to know that there is an entire atmosphere free of guilt, condemnation, and fear available to you! As a child of God, you are free to experience your Father and the life he dreamed about for you, with him and others. I promise that my journey will inspire you to not waste another moment in condemnation or fear. Sin has no hold on you! Not the sin of others nor the sin you may fall into. The spiritual life is meant to be our primary place of reality. And all that we experience in this natural realm must submit to that other reality when Kingdom-minded children of the Most-High God speak with the authority of their Father.

This habit of folding inward was not meant to be a place of "hiding from" but "being with." I think I was particularly better at that than all the other trauma reactions because of that long season of life where being grounded became so familiar to me.

I believe I spent so much of my early life grounded because my father found it impossible to love me. My birth certainly, seemed to be the cause of my mother's untimely death. I think that every time he looked at me, he saw her, and remembered her absence. Subconsciously, he had a wall of pain that prevented him from loving me as a child. I remember his harsh anger, and often avoided his attention for fear of being disciplined or encountering afresh his disapproval.

This void of affection and approval deeply affected my growth and development as a child. The abuse that was verbal, emotional, and physical sat like a nasty infected layer of additional pain on top of the sexual abuse I had previously experienced without my father's knowledge. It was a secret deep inside me and all this pain and rejection created a wounded place that constantly compelled me to comfort and protect myself. On occasion I would attempt to claw my way out of that wounded place with rage and wrath, fighting to the surface beyond the layers of labels of words spoken over me by others wrapping themselves around me like bandages that were too tight for proper healing. I would escape with grand exits and then begin to rebuild that cage of protection when I encountered again another situation full of fear and abuse. My love tank seemed to never get full. It couldn't. It had holes in it that leaked whatever went into it. Gradually over time, it would be empty and worse, full of muck. The residue of the wounds and the disappointments of others sat inside of me like a swamp of death and failure.

All my life I longed for affection and approval. I lived in a cloud of the fear of rejection, a sense of failing before I even tried, and a general desire to be comforted deeply. I did not receive that from others, so I took care of that myself. I suffered from an eating disorder from the age of 14. Binging on food was a way of comforting the needy spaces inside of me and lulling them to sleep. I would purge regularly out of guilt, trying to control my bad behavior. It was a crazy cycle that stayed with me until 1 was in my 30's. I also had other ways of trying to soothe the fears inside of me with alcohol, sex, masturbation, romance novels and endless hours watching television series that ran through my mind like diarrhea runs through the bowels. They offered me no sustenance or strength. They only added to my guilt.

The cycles of life would come and offer me a new opportunity to shine for someone else. I found new purpose in the calling to ministry. I would come to the aid of another's vision, never questioning why I had no vision for my own life. I submitted my void to their vision and found it fit quite nicely. When people were done with me and my acts of service, it was painful. I processed it as rejection. I did not realize that *every assignment of man has a time to start and a time to end*. When those endings came, they were often messy and full of tears no matter how much honor I showed to those around me. No act of service or care could keep them from being done with me.

What you do not know about yourself will have to bow to what others value you for once you add your agreement to their judgment. If their life is powerfully moving forward, you will become a part of their undertow if you have no personal visionary purpose for being there. You can't have that without a sense of assignment, of being sent on mission with authority, power, and purpose as God's emissary in the kingdom of God on the Earth! If there is no standard or main character development in the plot line of your life around your own purpose, you will not be the heroine or hero of your own story. You will merely be the sidekick or servant to the adventures of others.

It was in one of these places that my assignment began to shift, and in my weariness, I processed it as rejection. I found myself back in the depths of the secret place. But this time, I wasn't hiding. I was discovering the intertwining of God and me in a new and fresh way. Here I found myself physically very tired, spent spiritually, triggered in my soul and desperate for deeper places in God. I spent a year trying to encourage those who had set me aside into a new place of service that didn't quite fit to value me again. I was strong enough to know that I had value in God. I realized how my sense of destiny and calling was irrevocable tied to ministry and yet I could not imagine a life without that framework. I had a purpose in God, but it seemed that purpose had lost its fit in the life of the very ministry I worked in.

I could work in the trenches of people's souls, and it felt like low hanging fruit for the anointing on my life. Yet the new assignment I had I had been given, though it placed me in proximity to lots of people with lots of needs, only permitted me to lightly tend to their needs. So, I started a new practice separate from my ministry position so that I could spend time helping people get free from their overwhelming pain and find their identity in a fresh and living way. I loved it but it brought more discord to my ministry position than I imagined it could, especially with my leaders in my spiritual family. I tried desperately to understand what these relational changes meant to me personally and how they were affecting my faith journey.

In places where spiritual mothers and fathers are struggling with their identity you will also find a conglomerate of spiritual sons and daughters looking for affirmation. God did not answer all my questions then. But in that trying season, I became aware of the things that did matter in my own heart. I realized that though I had not had a great earthly parenting model, I had been deeply invested in parenting my own children and those of others. I had many spiritual sons and daughters who had grown in their relationship with God through the love, nurture, and guidance I had given them. My style of loving others that flowed out of the revelation of Father God's unconditional love for me was compelling. I loved not only those in my own church but also those in the community. I had other sons and daughters who had wounds that were afflicted on them by mothers and fathers. There were orphaned adults walking around bleeding while on mission for God. God would lead them to me, and I would walk with them. I would love them big as I got to know them, just as God loved them. I refused to know them only by their failures or needs but would call them out of sin into destiny. This ability was unlocked in me through an experience I have not shared publicly. But I am going to share it with you now.

In 2016, I was at a Global Awakening Conference. In a session with keynote speaker Bill Johnson, there was a place in the spirit realm we encountered where Pastor Bill did an amazing job of lingering in the atmosphere. During that time as he was facilitating what God was doing in the room, a young woman on the other side of the room screamed out, "It's because You love me so much that I have so much faith!" She was screaming loudly and weeping, and her words were hard to decipher. But I heard her clearly. Bill waited rather than try to move on. She then ran to the front of the room and looked up at him like a little girl and said "I am so sorry! I know I shouldn't have done that, but I am so overwhelmed right now! He loves me so much and that is why people are always asking me to pray for them. My prayers always work for others, but not for me. I know he loves them so much! I pray and it's like Heaven opens and helps them. But I didn't know that was the biggest sign of how much he loved *me*! He trusts me, but I could not see it!"

Bill graciously and calmly said, as she ran away back up an aisle, "Someone might want to follow her because she is in the middle of a revelation, and she is going to be overwhelmed by it and fall." Sure enough, she ran up the isle next to me and landed at the feet of the person on the end of my isle. As she landed, she said out loud, "I have great faith *because* I am greatly loved by my Father!" Her words penetrated me to my core! Remember my name? What she said was true for me, too. Like her, my prayers had great power in them but seemed blocked in my own life. I wept at the revelation that this was a demonstration of the deep abiding love of the Father in me and towards me. I asked him to show me more. He did!

In the next session Randy Clark held a powerful impartation session where he was laying hands on people who were experiencing manifestations of healing, tingling or heat in their body. My heart was to support him and study how he flowed in this powerful atmosphere of healing and activation in people's lives. He facilitated the anointing of God in the room. I was mesmerized. Suddenly, my head felt heavy, and I closed my eyes. As I did, an open vision appeared before me. I could still hear the room, but instead I saw a path like a dirt road in the country. It was green and lush and there was color everywhere. A man was walking towards me in the distance. He had long brown hair to his shoulders and a close-trimmed beard. He had on carpenter-style jeans and a flannel shirt.

In my head, I was astonished at what was happening! I thought to myself, "He looks like the Jesus movement version of Jesus!?" But I was joking to myself, and not really serious. Yet, even as I thought it, and the man grew closer, he tucked his hair behind his shoulders as he cocked it to the side and smiled broadly at me. I knew he had heard my thoughts and was responding to it. He responded to me. "It *is* me, Faith. I am here with you." I was shocked. "Why?" I asked. "How?" He replied, "Faith you asked our Father for more. I am here in response to that. For you have suffered a great absence of true brotherly love and affection. I have come to be with you. To be your big brother and walk with you and show you many things to come."

I then began to travel with him, still in the spirit. The last thing I remember was being in an airport setting with him. He was teaching me how to order and reorder the planes to send them off from the ground to new destinations. It was a deeply moving experience for me. As it ended, the atmosphere of the conference room became more real to me again. My friend touched my arm and asked if I was ready to leave. We had planned to get something to eat between the services. But she let me know that they were clearing the room for the next service now. We no longer had time for dinner. Though the entire experience seemed to have been about 10 minutes to me, it wasn't. I had been standing in that position for almost 2 hours! Frozen with my head back on my neck, my arms gently out and yet I was moving around with Jesus in the spirit realm!

As my friend and I exited the sanctuary, I felt heavy and was moving slowly. I sensed him right next to me still. He told me to pick up my feet and to stop acting weird! He said to me, "You didn't forget how to walk, and I am not weird. Nor am I going to make you weird so stop being weird and walk with me!" Man, was I trying, but I was so overwhelmed by my experience! I remember saying to my friend, "Jesus is right here at my side! Can you see him?" She was so gracious and respectful of my experience, saying "No I can't. But I believe you can." Jesus walked with me for some time after that. He was my big brother. There was a point where that tangible experience of him changed to be accepted companionship. He shared life with me then in a very practical and instructive way. My entire relationship with Father God and Jesus was deeply impacted by that experience.

Though I did not sense him in such a disruptive, tangible way as I did in the beginning of this visitation, I knew his presence was with me and could often sense him as if he talked in my ear while walking with me. I realized I had a family, a *real* family, that I was not tapping into as deeply as I could! Never despise an experience with God. Only he marks our life for eternity.

There were open wounds in my soul that were healed in those years that followed merely by being a part of that family and learning from his perspective how important the essence of family was to our Father. No matter the fallacies of men around me. No matter how they had tried to fill the gaps in my life and failed, I was okay! I was able to give them grace for their struggles with relationship, even when they unintentionally hurt me in the process. It was then that God began to cause me to recognize the value of those I had relationship with all over the globe that were not my natural family but were so much a part of my life. They prayed for me, laughed with me and we learned from each other all the time. He also introduced me to a new tribe of people who revered family and faith in a way that caused my senses to come alive again. In meeting them I realized how many relationships I had developed over the years that were significant and purposefully outside of the local ministry I served in.

Never underestimate the power of the pull of a global community of faith-filled believers to the wounded soul. These new friends were not my natural family. But they became my spiritual family. I could trust them as leaders, because they were a family looking to grow their family with more sons and daughters. They were not talking about numbers or programs. They talked about their spiritual sons and daughters in the light of their callings and destiny as if they were their own children with great gifts and skills. All their context was around the knowledge they had of them as individuals that God had called to their family. They embraced me in the same way and began to get to know the design of God in me. They didn't elevate my wounds above my passion for God.

I found acceptance and the love of God for his family was demonstrated to me there. To some, I am a mother. To others, a daughter. To me, this is my spiritual family. The ones who feel responsible to know me and grow with me. They let me into their life by being authentic and true with me. They share their fallacies and their follies. They also share their gold nuggets of wisdom from Father God. More so, they share how they got those nuggets from Him. They regularly invite me into their own journey of growth and discovery. It wasn't such a mysterious thing that I couldn't hope to find the path myself. They showed me the ways that God speaks to them, teaching them and correcting them. They became low hanging fruit for me, bowing their own discoveries of God to me in such a way that I could climb up and discover them myself. This is the family life that God desires for those who have been born into the Kingdom of God. This framework of family is meant to emit such a fragrance of His love when they are together, it compels others to join our Father's family.

I began to not just yearn for the fragrance of Father's love for me, but I became a bearer of the same scent. I opened my life to the genuine move of God that celebrates the journey to healing and restoration even as it champions the nature of Christ in each believer. I settled into life with this amazing group of sons and daughters of God. I learned what it was to live as a daughter of the Most High. My spiritual father's unconditional love opened a new place in my heart to receive the unconditional love of the Father for me in a fresh and living way.

Life Application

1. In what ways have you encountered truth about God? Share one that was particularly personal to you.

2. How have the wounds you have experienced from others who also love Jesus affected your faith?

3. What examples for loving family has God placed in your life?

4. Do you know what it means to be a son or daughter of God?

5. How do you want to grow in your revelation of spiritual family? Ask God to open up that revelation to you and to bring people into your life that love you and see you as family.

Chapter Four
SONS AND DAUGHTERS

It is your faith that we support and encourage that expands the kingdom mission. We must get to know you, or we will not know what your faith is in you for. The Church is not meant to develop programs for people to find their fit in. The people have the programs in them. The mission belongs to them. Our job is to find the joy of equipping you with what you lack so you can find the same joy in being who and what you are called to be. (2 Corinthians 1:24; Ephesians 4:12)

—Christopher Scarinzi

I have never experienced anything sweeter than being blessed to find a new family who valued the experience of relationship as much as I did. My first encounter with my spiritual dad, Chris Scarinzi was at a table full of appetizers laid out by a wonderful couple who invited a diverse group of pastors across Central New York to their home. He was expounding on a passage of scripture as he often can be found doing. Here is what he shared that grabbed my heart:

> *Not that we have dominion over your faith but*
> *are fellow workers for your joy; for by faith, you*
> *stand.*
>
> **—2 Corinthians 1:24**

Pastor Chris began to explain that it is not the responsibility of the leaders of the church family to dominate the calling of their sheep by telling them where to serve, how to live, or what to be. Instead, he offered for consideration, that in this passage Apostle Paul is saying that it was the early apostles' goal to walk along side of their people in such a way that they would know them personally - their calling, purpose, strengths, and weaknesses. They could work with them as "fellow workers" so that they would individually fulfill the goal or purpose of God's measure of faith within them. In doing so, both the leader and those they were leading would experience great joy.

This communal mission is being accomplished through the deep *knowing* of each individual. This is the exact opposite of the denominations or faith movements I have encountered and studied in the world today. Most ministries want people to know the vision of the church and serve the greater vision of a man of God with their own. It is the congregant's responsibility to figure out how that works and the way to best do that is by plugging in and serving others. This new attitude that Pastor Chris portrayed that day of the leader serving the sheep and getting to know them so that they walk in the fullness of their calling was so compelling for me! He went on to explain to me over dinner that evening that it was not the purpose of a church to have a mission program to impact the world that came only from one couple who birthed all the vision, but for the leaders to equip the callings of those who came alongside of them by helping them to discover the purpose and provision for the vision God had put in them. Hence, instead of having a mission's program that sent out teams, those in our family who God called to foreign and domestic soils for a specific purpose would be equipped with the finances, knowledge, training, and spiritual support so that they would be successful and full of joy in the doing of it. This requires us to know those whom God sends us, to know their strengths and their weaknesses. It requires us to not draw back from those weaknesses but to come alongside them in those places for the purpose of helping them find new wisdom and strength in God. Oh, how my heart sang with the truth of this scripture he was sharing! To be a child of this eternal family is to be called to greatness and I began to feel its stirrings in me that day!

Romans 6:23 declares that each person who commits their life to God receives the free gift of unbroken eternal relationship with Him. Through the work of Jesus, we have been set free from the curse of sin that separated us from our Father. All our debts mentioned in Romans 6:23 which accrued from our bondage to sin have been paid off! Yet this is not all we receive in that exchange! When we surrender our old life to receive a new one, we get a gift! It is a seed - carrying the same DNA as Jesus Himself! We have the same seed of greatness in us as Jesus did Himself! We often refer to Jesus as, Jesus Christ, as if this is his first and last name. But it is simply a reference to Jesus as The Christ. Galatians 3:16 declares:

"Now to Abraham and his seed were the promises made. He does not say, "And to seeds," as of many, but speaks of one, "And to your seed," who is Christ."

In the Greek, it is referencing the "Christos seed"[2] or "the anointed seed"[3]. In verse 19 it speaks of the law being a servant until the "seed" promised to Abraham came, who is Christ. His name is Jesus the Christ. He is the first anointed seed. He carried the first seed of Christ in human form so that He could prove forever that God and Man were meant to be one. He will forever be the first to bear the seed of Christ.

For this, God declares in Philippians 2:9 that Jesus has been exalted to the highest place and given the name that is above or before every other name. He is the first of a long line of others born again to be like Him. We are sons and daughters of the same family line. The work that the Father and Jesus accomplished was for a family line, not just one son. When you receive that gift of freedom from sin, God the Father births in you a brand-new spirit in the form of a seed - an anointed seed – carrying his own DNA. Galatians 3:6-9 tells us that it is not just the seed of a man, Abraham. It is the very seed of Christ! The implantation of this "Christos seed" is not merely endowed as a gift given to us. It is a condition of something new being birthed in us.

Jesus replied, "Very truly I tell you, no one can see the kingdom of God unless they are born again"

—John 3:3

Therefore, if anyone is in Christ, he is a new creation; old things have passed away; behold, all things have become new.

—2 Corinthians 5:17

In John 3, Jesus tells Nicodemus that to be a part of this new Kingdom you must not only be born out of a woman's natural birthing of a child through the mother's placental water, but you must receive the second birth of the spirit. You must be "born-again" into the Kingdom family. This is where the term "a born-again Christian" originates.

I was not merely created. I was birthed – once by my mother, and again, by the Spirit of God. My body has a house of flesh and bone but it's what is inside that body that carries my true image. I was sired at that moment by Father God and his seed was implanted in me. This new birthing supersedes the old one in such a way that it provides me with access to spiritual truths and realities we are still coming to know and understand! I am not merely a mortal being with flesh; I am a supernatural daughter of what scripture calls God, the Father of Lights and Perfections (James 1:17). If you have experienced this new birth, you now have the very DNA of God himself inside of you in seed form! Like Jesus, you are a walking, living expression of the glory of God on the Earth. We sing in so many Christian songs about the glory of God covering the Earth. The word for *glory* is the Greek word "doxa"[4] which means literally "the reputation" of a thing. We are those vessels who cover the Earth with the reputation of God and emit the fragrance of life to those seeking life.

> *For we are the aroma of Christ to God among those who are being saved and among those who are perishing, to one a fragrance from death to death, to the other a fragrance from life to life.*
>
> **—2 Corinthians 2:14-15**

But here is the really troubling question that must be asked. How on Earth can this be true considering all the brokenness and sin upon the Earth? In Hosea 4:6, God says that His people perish for lack of knowledge. Isaiah 53:6 says that the Earth is full of those who are like sheep led astray without a shepherd. There are many false shepherds in the Earth today. But even more heartbreaking is the fact that there are good men and women who are children of God called to shepherd, but out of brokenness and personal deception, they are leading sheep into their own vision and desires for greatness. With great schemes for impact, they trade the influence gifted to them from God for mere goals that match the business models of corporate America today. This does not satisfy men nor fulfill

God's heart for his family to impact the Earth with power and cover it with the knowledge of his reputation.

Inside of each of person who has accepted the gift of new life through faith in Jesus, is a seed meant to propagate and overtake the Earth with the goodness of God. Isn't it interesting, that this all comes in the form of a seed? The concept of seedtime and harvest is all throughout the Bible in the old and new testaments. Every new life starts with a seed. Yet, the death of a seed, as described in John 12:24, appears to be an equally important part of the process of the seed's lifecycle and purpose. In order for it to bear the fruit written in the code of its DNA, it must first fall into the ground and suffer a process like death. A farmer would tell you that the hard shell hosting the DNA cracks open in the darkness. It is the shell containing the seed that actually dies a death. This allows what is hidden within it to begin to come forth and grow as it receives the nutrients of the soil around it. In the same way we receive the new life through a seed. The DNA of God is placed into the very midst of our own spirit and as it cracks open, a tree of life begins to transform your life as you grow in Christ.

I want to take a moment to talk about this amazing seed. It's anointed, incorruptible and eternal in its nature. It is not just the answer to our sin condition prior to the new birth. It is a tree of eternal life springing up out of the eternally flowing "waters" of the spirit realm. (John 4:14) This is the second birth that Nicodemus in John 3 failed to value. In Matthew 16:16, there is a very famous text where Peter answers Jesus when asked, "Who do you say that I am?" Peter replies, "You are the **Christ**, the son of the Living God." The following reply of Jesus indicates that there is something about Peter's statement that is so profound, only the Father himself could have revealed it to Peter. Furthermore, whatever that is, will become the very foundation of the body being built up into the "ecclesia" which is the Greek word we later translated to church. Ecclesia simply means, "the assembling together of the called-out ones. This will be such a strong foundation with so much power, that the very gates of hell will not stand against this powerful influencing kingdom known as The Church.

> *Jesus answered and said to him, "Blessed are you, Simon Bar-Jonah, for flesh and blood has not revealed this to you, but My Father who is in Heaven. And I also say to you that you are Peter, and on this rock, I will build My church, and the gates of Hades shall not prevail against it. And I will give you the keys of the kingdom of Heaven, and whatever you bind on Earth will be bound in Heaven, and whatever you loose on Earth will be loosed in Heaven." Then he commanded His disciples that they should tell no one that he was Jesus the Christ.*
>
> **—Matthew 16:16–20**

We see here in this passage that Jesus, is revealed by Peter to be the Anointed Seed - the Christ. This was very significant because the holy scriptures through the ages had spoken of a seed that would be birthed out of the lineage of King David. The church would be built not on Jesus the man, but on the seed of Christ that was in him. He was literally the first of that seed to walk the Earth, but there would be many more! Romans 8:29 declares that Jesus was the firstborn amongst many brethren to come. The Church is designed to be a family birthed out of an anointed seed - that "Christos seed" of God that would carry His own DNA. That seed would have within it the power or capacity to break open and become a tree of life with much fruit! This seed of Christ is an invasive species! It has the power to take over an entire person's soul and body with such a ferocity, if allowed, that no habit will be left unchanged, no thought left unprovoked, no disease left to grow, or calling undiscovered. If you have given your life to God, you have received the same seed that was in Jesus.

There are too many "Pickled Christians" today. They are anointed and called with great destiny but have been placed on a shelf by leaders who believed that they would grow under the watchful hand of time. But I call them "pickled" because they exude a bitterness from being on the sidelines for too long. They have not been placed in conditions that would cause that seed to break open and begin to invade their life. They often can be found sitting not just on the sidelines, but also in the thick of serving. All the while, the hide their issues and pain from the eyes of those they serve with under the guise of holiness or excellence. They long for recognition and affirmation, but they grow tart and sassy with leaders and others around them. We fail to activate their calling by refusing to push them out of the nest and into the adventure of Kingdom life. They fail to encounter spiritual mothers and fathers who get to know them and see in them the greatness of that seed. They fail to grow into spiritual fathers and mothers themselves. I have had the privilege of spiritually parenting several sons and daughters. In ministry life, I would often be given the ones that were too messy for others – too needy, unrefined, or broken to be quickly turned into something useful for service. They would often come to me with great bleeding wounds inflicted upon them in areas of their life where they were already bleeding and needed help but were harshly disciplined instead. If you don't get to know someone, you might misinterpret their behavior or responses to you incorrectly. You can't *discipline* pain away. When we take this approach, we miss the opportunity to know the true worth and value God saw in sending that person to us. He sends us valuable assets, but we often see messes that need to be cleaned up. Wounds from other Christians would linger with infection in the soul of these precious people. "How is it we can be so mean to each other in the Church," I would reason. Yet, if we do not see the value of every single man or woman to God as what they truly are, the seed of Christ, we will be easily moved by all the negative labels with which life and the enemy have labeled them. C.S. Lewis said this:

> *There are no ordinary people. You have never met a mere mortal. …It is a serious thing to live in a society of possible gods and goddesses, to remember that the dullest and most uninteresting*

person you can talk to may one day be a creature which, if you saw it now, you would be strongly tempted to worship, or else a horror and a corruption such as you now meet, if at all, only in a nightmare.[5]

God created humanity to become a family with an eternal destiny to rule and reign with Him in life and death. You are a son or daughter with a mighty calling and purpose on your life. Your Father is the same God who holds eternity and time in the palm of His hand. Can you hear destiny beckoning to you? Can you choose to accept that despite what failures you may see in your life to this point, or even your successes, if you are born again, the seed of God's purpose in you is cracking open and growing in you right now. You were designed for greatness, just like Jesus! Can you imagine that those around you may be also? If these things are brand new to you and you feel overwhelmed by the potential of these words, then the fragrance of life is drifting out of this book into your heart, enticing you with its possibilities. Take a moment to receive that new birth experience. Surrender your life to Father God and simply receive the work of Jesus Christ in your heart.

Just say "Yes, I receive you as my Father, God. I believe Jesus died for me. I receive the finished work of Jesus Christ for me. Break open that seed of Christ in me that I might be changed forever." This gift is not just an exit strategy from the bonds of sin and death. It is a gift of eternal life through sonship. It is to become like Jesus - capable of living a life free from sin. It is to receive the power to choose life with each and every breath, to walk this Earth in light of the fact that an eternal purpose is at work in your life. You are not lost, without hope or purpose. No matter what condition your life appears to be in, everything at this moment is subject to change. Your dreams are valid. Your hopes have purpose. Your life is significant. No one else can do what you are designed to do, be what you are designed to be. You are not alone in this discovery. The same spiritual power that was in Jesus is in you. You are supernatural. You are not merely human. You are YOU... Just like Jesus!

Life Application

1. How has God called you to greatness?

2. Are you surrounded by those who see your value and encourage its growth in you?

3. How is your growth and maturity being discovered and developed?

4. Are you busy serving the vision of someone else that your own vision is being overlooked, underdeveloped?

5. Pray and ask God to reveal your identity to you. Sit with Him and meditate on Psalm 139:14 that declares you are fearfully and wonderfully made. Read 2 Corinthian 1:24 and ask yourself what the faith of God is in you for. Let the spirit of God bring clarity to you. The spirit of God is in you to guide you and help you fulfill your purpose.

Chapter Five
JUST LIKE JESUS

We are his dream come true! We are not the in-vention of our parents! You are the greatest idea God has ever had!

—**Francois DuToit**

For so many years of my life I tried to be something I already was. I tried to not be an addict in the hidden spaces. To be free from wrong thinking. To feel accepted, not rejected. To be whole and not broken. I tried out eve-rything I was taught. ***But trying only gets you religion with rules, not lasting freedom***. I had to receive the com-pletely new birth that Jesus spoke to Nicodemus about in John 3:1-21. To experience the Kingdom lifestyle of this new family you must be born again. Trying so hard on my own was unessential once I had become new. To be reborn as a new creature gives me access to everything my Father has! The Mirror Translation of John 3:7 has a footnote by Francois DuToit saying, "We are his dream come true! We are not the invention of our parents! You are the great-est idea God has ever had!"[6] Yes, we have been born in the flesh through our mother's womb. But this new birth is a work of the Spirit. Christ is not given to you as a gift to figure out or work out in the flesh. It is a condition of a new birth that takes place in your spirit, by God's Spirit. A seed of Christ - God's own DNA is deposited in you. And according to Galatians 3:16, it is given to as many as receive this promise of freedom from sin-likeness to Godlikeness through faith in Jesus. Hebrews 2:11 declares that both he who rescued us from sin, as well as those he rescued originate from the same source. Because of this he is not ashamed to call us his family. He does not lord his glory over us; he invites us into the same glory (Hebrews 2:10)!

When we receive by faith the gift of "salvation," or new birth that Jesus was inviting Nicodemus to experience, we are rescued out of the sin-conscious lifestyle into a Kingdom family with a new set of DNA that guarantees our sonship! We cry out "Abba Father" from within (Galatians 4:6; Romans 8:15). That cry is meant to live within us for life. It unlocks the promised family inheritance of the new covenant that God spoke into Abraham 430 years before the law was even established through Moses! The old covenant law reined in sin's capacity to completely destroy man but in no way fulfilled the judgment against sin. Jesus came into the Earth and fulfilled the requirement of the law perfectly and settled the judgement or penalty for sin once and for all time! In fulfilling the work of the Law, Jesus proved a man could fulfill every single working of the law through the accompanying nature of the divine within him. Jesus not only dealt with man's bondage to sin, but he walked in complete victory, opening the door for us to do the same! By faith in Jesus' finished work against sin, and with God's abiding presence in our lives, we too can choose to live free of sin. We get to choose life as sons or daughters of God, every single day! How? Let's look at a powerful scripture in Galatians:

This is what God had in mind all along: the blessing He gave to Abraham might extend to all nations through the Anointed One, Jesus; and we are the beneficiaries of this promise of the Spirit that comes only through faith.

—Galatians 3:14 (VOICE)

Just like Jesus, we have access through the spirit of God to the anointing, relationally and positionally. This anointing is the power of God emanating from within that seed-of-Christ-life. It is the divine power of God that comes from the supernatural realm. That anointing is invisible but has visible impact on the natural realm. To be anointed is to be a conduit between the invisible realm and the visible one. It is to deliver Heavenly possibilities into the impossibilities on the Earth. It is the stuff of miracles, signs, and wonders. As we become one with the Father, we are given the power to live a life connected in oneness with the spirit realm - the eternal realm – his Kingdom. We have the same power to demonstrate God's heart on the Earth that Jesus had! He desires for people to see us, and thereby see him. When faced with challenges, we are meant to retreat from that old way of responding, and instead yield to a new cry of our heart, "Father, what do you say about this?" I don't know about you, but I am still reeling from this revelation and asking God to give me the same mind that Jesus had in relationship to His Father.

So many times, in the short life of Jesus recorded in scripture, we see Him getting away to spend time with His Father. The secret place was not just His hiding place; it was His strengthening and aligning space. In this place, between his Father and him, he was aligned correctly for what was and was coming yet. He was so dependent on this relational space that he said to Phillip in John 14:7-14, "If you have seen me, you have seen the Father! So, stop asking me to see Him! We are one. My Words are His and the authority by which I speak is directly related to my relationship in Him! Locationally and relationally, we are ONE!" *(my paraphrase)* Our issue is that we see ourselves as "mere humans" rather than the sons and daughters of God that the Earth is crying out for and earnestly expecting in Romans 8:19. We do not recognize the power of the seed of God's DNA inside of us, nor its capacity to break open and produce a tree of life. The fruit and leaves of this spiritual tree interact with this natural realm, still held in the grip of those in bondage to sin.

In my life, my inability to recognize my value was a huge stumbling block and it opened a door to so much sin in my life; my own sin and the sin of others against me. When you don't know your value, you will be willing to try anything that promises you something better. My life was imprinted at a very early age with the invasive emotional and physical violence of sexual abuse. As a result, my mind believed that my value came from meeting the needs of other people. I was often used and then carelessly put aside. Even after receiving that new life in Christ, it was contained inside of a broken woman who believed her identity came from her value to others. I had to learn that I had incredible value to God himself. As I grew in the culture I described earlier, so rich with the word of God, I began to know and understand that I had a different identity, a divine identity, inside. But the two seemed at war within me!

What you don't know to be true, can keep you busy fighting things that God has already defeated for you in those moments I would wonder about the truth of the word of God. Did it really have the power to save me? Heal me? Deliver me? I saw my life as a series of events of transformation where old information was being exchanged for new. The knowledge of God himself became so engrained in me, it began to affect the way I saw my own design. Yet it still was not enough to really help me to understand that I was actually free! According to Romans 6:22, I already been set free from slavery to sin! Not just to be now a "slave" to God, but for every *separation* from him to be removed so that I would produce everything from a place of oneness with him! The word for *sin* in the Greek is "hamartia"[7]. It means to miss the mark, or to aim for something else but to not hit what you were aiming for. Many who are in bondage to sin are misdirected in their aim because they have been blindfolded by the sins of generations that lived before them.

In Romans 6, Paul used the only relationship he recognized in culture that day that was bonding and binding to describe our oneness with God - slavery. He saw the bondage of slavery to sin and knew those he was writing to would also. But the word translated as *slavery* to God in the Greek actually means every degree of separation having been removed so that you are irrevocably linked to God himself without any capacity to do anything without him anymore.[8] In Paul's culture, the only time a man would lose his own freedom is when he is bound to another man's freedoms. Slavery to anything is the antithesis to the freedom we are meant to find in God!

Though Paul addresses himself as a "slave" or "servant" to Christ in Romans 1:1, the Greek word translated as *slave* is "doulos," and it depicts one who willingly lives under the authority of another. To live under authority is to live inside of the scope of, or influence of another one who is authorized over the territory you occupy.[9] We now live under the authority of Christ. In Galatians 5:1, Paul tells us that it is for freedom that we have been set free! So, don't buy into a new type of bondage slavery and become enslaved again! Be free – be one with the Father instead! Paul was crying out in Romans to his "children," the churches he birthed and helped to grow. He was in that awful place every parent eventually faces when their children leave home. Wondering if they will live the way that you taught them to live. Or if they will become entrenched in culture and forget their roots and all they learned from you? What an awkward season for young adults as they discover the purpose of freedom in a new way.

This freedom Paul writes about is meant to be our introduction to the Father's way of life. It is an introduction to a family life inside a kingdom that is vibrant and alive with victory over sin and evil. An invitation to know our Father and big brother Jesus in such a way that we choose every day to guard and protect our freedom by *not* partaking in the immoral nature of sin that mankind so enjoys. We have been given the keys to victory over sin in our own life, but they are keys that are of a family nature. If I give my car keys to my daughter to drive my car, she can drive it! But if she breaks into the neighbor's house and steals his keys to drive his car, we have a problem! The privileges and benefits of family are far more gracious and satisfying than taking something that doesn't belong to us from a stranger! Yet, we live our lives too often out of this reality. We are trying to take something that doesn't belong to us, but we want to possess. I know I operated that way. Maybe you too?

We don't have to try and get it. We have family privileges, but we must accept them and be family with God and each other. Going back to that passage in Romans 6:22-23 describe to us what it means to have every degree of separation removed between us and our Father.

But now having been set free from sin, and having become slaves of God, you have your fruit to holiness, and the end, everlasting life. For the wages of sin is death, but the gift of God is eternal life in Christ Jesus our Lord.

It is so powerful - the holiness or wholeness of our eternal condition with a Holy God! We have already been gifted this. We are not in bondage to sin anymore. We have received eternity, now! And all of his nature is ours! We are like our Poppa!

So many believers speak his Word, but their authority does not come from a vibrant relationship with their Father and so they have very little real power. Authority without true power is always an indicator of a man who does not know his Father intimately. He does not know the privilege of his family name. To be even more watchful of is a man who has great power and authority but no love in his words. One who can quote scripture and answer every question with it, yet there is more passion for the judgement and wrath of God than God's deep love for mankind. A man or woman focused on condemnation and judgment is of a different father. For our enemy has power also. his words can be compelling, and he is not afraid to use scripture in his arguments. After all, he also spoke scripture to Jesus in the wilderness, didn't he (Matthew 4)? Yet without love, we are a clanging cymbal, or noisemaker (1 Corinthians 13). For all his power and noisiness, this person is doing nothing of the Kingdom's work. For only Love gives power a clarion sound of authority that brings glory and fruit to the true Father.

Only in knowing God the Father as Jesus did, as a son, can we ever hope to live a life as he did. Jesus is the absolute trophy of God! He proved that a man can live in the flesh without sinning, if the spirit of God is in him. I want to be just like Jesus - free of sin. I want to live a life of vital eternal union with God the Father in the Spirit? Don't you? The truth is, we can!

Life Application

1. How has the rules of religion superseded your relational rights in God's family?

2. Do you get your value in any way from other people?

3. How has your belief system about yourself been changed as you find your value in God's eyes and written word?

4. Do you believe that you have the ability to live sin free? Why might that seem hard for you?

5. Write a letter to yourself encouraging yourself to believe that you are a child of God saved from the issue of sin. Be open about the obstacles you see to that. Find scriptures to respond to those obstacles.

Chapter Six
BOLDNESS TO BE ME

All this is proceeding along lines planned all along by God and then executed in Christ Jesus. When we trust in him, we're free to say whatever needs to be said, bold to go wherever we need to go.

—**Ephesians 3:11** (VOICE)

If there was one condition that I have been guilty of, it is this - a lack of boldness. I think everyone desires a dose of it. And doesn't it seem like some people have gotten an extra dose of it with birth? There are many teachings, courses, coaches to hire and ways of gaining boldness. But those are not how I gained boldness. Remember when I said earlier that I was surrounded by amazing teachers and mentors? I would mimic them like a good child, or better yet, like a good disciple. I feel like so much of my life was spent that way. I remember as a teenager buying my dad a poster at a school sale that I thought he would love. Let's just say: He. Did. Not. Love. It! It said, "There are only two ways to do things. My way and the wrong way." That was my perception of my dad. I thought he was comfortable with this as a life philosophy. Apparently, he wasn't. I literally never learned how to think for myself as a child.

I was never allowed to, never taught to think through and solve a problem. I was dependent on the decision making of others. I was told how to do everything, and there was only one right way to do it. It was a harsh reality for someone as creative as me. Secretly, I would formulate other ways to accomplish or say something. Yet, I learned early on that to speak it out loud or to try and change the "right way" was a dangerous move with great repercussions.

This silencing of my voice, the muffling of my will to choose well, and the stifling of my gifts and talents was nearly fatal in my life. I became someone who was a vague, powerless, walking ghost. I was a pale echo of everyone else's voice. My own was only championed in times of crisis as it would rise to the challenge in those times, manifesting strategies that would lead the way through and out for others. Then at other times, like the prophet Jeremiah, I would find myself in a pit at the hands of others, having spoken truth they didn't want to hear after being given a platform to speak. My words were often met with frustration and anger and would sometimes even bring out the worst in people.

I remember being ordained as a minister and in the prayer, my pastor prophesying over me that I would agitate demonic, human and regional authorities. Both angelic and demonic beings would be agitated to action by me. Boy, have I lived that word out! Internally, I felt that my voice was never really valued. Yet, as God drew me close and began to heal the wounds from my first family and all the failed family attempts since, I began to find my voice again. It was confusing because when my voice echoed the voices of others, it was valued. Looking at my life you might see value in the times I preached before people or taught in classrooms. But even then, I felt that I was mimicking others. It was only in the prayer place that I truly felt the freedom to experience the fullness of my spirit and its equipping for my life. I was an echo of God's voice in those spaces. Because I was falling in love with Him so deeply, I often had a soft and compelling sound to my prayer language. I began to get critical feedback about my "style" of prayer, saying it was too soft, intimate, prophetic, and not easily understood by others. My teaching style was too story-like or ethereal, and not as structured or as well prepared as others around me. And I listened to that feedback. I tailored my voice and gifts for men. I tried not to sound like a daughter speaking to her Father.

I became a general. My authority grew bolder. My teaching notes more developed. Yet, inside I was beginning to feel dry and void of love. No doubt I could pray for others and carry a room full of people into prayer, like a tour guide of the spirit realm. Yet, I sometimes felt like I lacked a depth that I knew was open to me personally. I felt often that I stopped at a threshold, whether in the Spirit or in a room full of powerful men and women of God. I would waiver with uncertainty about whether I had a right to be there. I felt unsure in my life, and yet I felt secure in Father's love. It was very confusing for me. I wished to be shed of the gift of leadership, of all the influence I had, and began longing for the affirmation of man again. Why couldn't I just fit in!?

Then I had an experience that changed that feeling forever.

In the fall a few years ago, I was invited to speak at another church. I felt like I was given a curious liberty. The church I was invited to said, "We acknowledge your prophetic gifts and your teaching gifts. We give you permission to be you. We believe God has birthed a message in you that is unusual, and specific for us, and this region. Say and do whatever is in your heart to do. We receive the word of the Lord from you." Matthew 10:41 speaks of a reward that comes to those who receive a prophet in the name or office of the prophet. The reward is the message the prophet brings. Because of this liberty, the word of the Lord to the people was rich that night. I ministered in this very powerful engaging space where I felt that all my purpose was being poured out in that room.

The message was simple, yet profound. During it, I took a water bottle that was set there for me to sip from as I ministered. It was my spirit inspired by God's Spirit that picked up that bottle in that moment. I didn't need a sip; I needed a physical object as a tool to demonstrate something very powerful and deep. God intended to pour out understanding in that room. I partook in it, even as it came out of me. I have repeated this exercise a few times since then and it never ceases to compel my spirit to tears, at the truth contained within it. This is what I shared as I held that water bottle. Keep in mind as you read on, the water bottle's form represents a container we call "The Church". The water bottle's style of cap and labels define what is inside that bottle to convince us of its value and entice us to partake of it. Like in scripture, the water itself inside the bottle represents the spirit realm and the cleansing word of God.

Get that picture in your mind as you read on. The bottle, the label, and cap all support functionally, to help us know what is in the bottle, and to get access to the contents. These three elements became elements of a prophetic parable that day.

The issue with the church in this generation we have been developed in is that they have grown a very fine appreciation for the containers or church buildings by which we have given people access to the things of the word and the spirit. The water in the bottle is representative of the Spirit life and the power of the Word of God therein. We select churches and ministries in the same way we go to a store to buy a bottle of water out of the cooler. We select the water we drink based on the labels on the bottles, the cap style that suits us best, flavors or electrolytes added to it, how pure it is versus how cheap, or how easily accessible the cap style makes it. The days of wells or filling a large container from a natural spring are a distant memory for most.

In the same way, we spend a ton of time in the church talking about our buildings, our doctrines, our style of worship or teaching, the extra media resources we use to enhance the experience and so much more. We all know the purpose of the bottle is the water inside of it, but we have lots of options for how we access that water. And so, we dicker about containers and styles and even share our right to choose with the staff or leadership of those who bottle the water and sell it to us.

Churches today are overdeveloped and under experienced in the Spirit, a mile wide and an inch deep in their understanding of the Spirit, driven by doctrine that divides and programs that enhance. Yet, they are curiously void of youth as if our own hunger has not reproduced a hunger in the next generation. They appear to be looking for water in other places. And that disturbs us immensely as the generation, who traditionally inherited a deep value for the container. It is a primary means of accessing this precious resource.

Here is the challenge we have today. There is a generation we have birthed that is not interested in all the styling of the bottles and containers. They are just thirsty! They were born thirsty and just want the water itself. They instinctively know they were born to partake of what we dole out to them carefully and thoughtfully. So many of them are like Psalm 42:1 "As the deer pants for the water brooks, so pants my soul for You, O God." They are so thirsty for the true and authentic experience of the invisible realm and its power that they bypass the process we were told we must honor, to trust our experience. We ourselves spend so much time talking about the bottle or container of the church and convincing them that our container is the best one for them. They are looking at us as if we were crazy, saying, "I think I can do what you are doing. Why are you trying to help me figure it out? I don't care for that bottle so much as you do. I care about the water inside. I know that water is available to me outside of that container you are handing to me!?" And so, they search for and choose water for themselves. They disdain the value of the containers, labels, designer experiences, and instead they search for water, drink deeply when they find it and share it loosely and casually - even at times mixing the profane in with the holy. Yet because we have lived before them with such an honor for the container, and not demonstrated the joy of drinking the water itself to them, they fail to go any deeper, to indulge their thirst with water unlimited in supply!

Jesus said to the woman at the well in John 4 that what he had to offer her was a wellspring of water that would never run dry. It was to be explored and sought after! Have you ever sought-after God, so hungry for more that you discovered the truth Jesus explained to that woman? You can never reach the bottom or end of God! his love, power, and truth are endless, and we are built with a desire for the deep places of God.

The last thing I said that day was more shocking than the rest. By the Spirit, I said that the most alarming fact we are unaware of. A new generation is being birthed *now* that was designed solely for the life of the waters of the spiritual realm. They are equipped to swim in it and experience it in extraordinary ways. They have an enhanced, supernatural ability to facilitate its movements with their own bodies, spirits, and souls. And yet because we don't recognize them for this amazing capacity, they are largely being undeveloped. In fact, in my opinion they are being medicated, labeled with ADD, ODD, autism, etc. The enemy is harnessing them with video games, avatars, virtual realities and guided artificial intelligence, and we are avoiding them. We need them to be "normal" and function in classrooms with many others. We don't recognize their spiritual gifts are active at birth. I have also noticed that there is an extraordinary number of children with the active gift of discerning of spirits. They are unusual in personality and focus. They don't fit well because they are not understood and therefore, not cultivated. They are born for the water but settle for swimming in cesspools of video games and pornography as means of escaping our dysfunctional understanding of their design. Their sweet precious identity is forced into molds that better fit our current styles of culture. The word of the Lord to us that night has never left my spirit and continues to develop in me. Here is what happened next. This truth produced a personal experience for me that changed me forever.

After the service, a young girl of 14 flitted around me like a butterfly until I asked her if she wanted to speak to me. She had left the room three times and continued to come back and put herself in my sight. She softly said, "Yes." She took me aside and said that she had a gift of being able to sense when spiritual beings are in the room but rarely could see them physically. She can sense angels in the service at times, but she said that night she saw a very large angel standing behind me as I ministered. He was in armor with wings out and alert during that time that I ministered. He was full of light and the light was shining around me as I ministered in a brilliant manner. She said there was another being that was female that was up off to the left of me and seemed to be watching me.

Now here is where I will let you have a peek into how the doctrines of men can be so dangerous to our Spirit life. I immediately thought to myself inside, "Well the Bible clearly does not talk about female angels so this girl and everything she said is not of the Lord." I began to do the friendly smile we afford people when we think they are crazy, but we don't want to offend them. My pride took over for a minute until the Lord spoke audibly in my spirit. He said, "This woman she is describing is not an angel! It is your mother. I have allowed her to see you minister this evening and her pride in you is something I want you to feel. I want you to feel my own affirmation and that of your mother's." The overwhelming truth of what He was saying to me washed over me. I almost crumbled in tears, completely shook by what he shared and what he poured out in that moment. I turned my face to the wall for a moment to just block out the noise in the room and feel completely what was washing over me. The delight of the Lord and his love for me was so tangible! The knowledge that he had allowed my mother to see me from the hidden realm in such a way that a young girl would see her watching me was overwhelming.

It took me 2 hours to leave the building after this conversation. I was shaken to my core by affirmation, identification, and parental love. For a woman who had never met her mother, because of her untimely death, to know she had been seen, known, and loved at that moment by her and by God himself. Wow! And this moment never would have happened without that young girl – a representative of the next generation and their unusual spiritual abilities. That wrecked all my shame, and even my doubts about my design. I am called to teach from the prophetic place. I am called to activate generations after me. And yes, my voice does agitate the demonic and cause angels to stand near me. In that moment of time, the very things I had preached about our identity being tied to an understanding and reverence for the spirit realm became so real for me. I heard and experienced the power God in the Spirit.

A lack of boldness is a sign that you have the Holy Spirit of God in your life, but He doesn't have all of you. My propensity to mistrust myself and God in me was evil. I trusted leaders more than I trusted him. My hunger for affirmation from my parents had mutated into a continual desire for affirmation from men and women who appeared parental to me. I am a champion of mentors and coaches who help people become a better version of themselves. But beware of those who want you to be like them.

We are called only to be like our Father. True spiritual parents get to know you in all your strengths, weaknesses, and failures. They encourage, build up and correct with truth in their hearts - the truth of God's design that is uniquely expressed in you. That takes time and investment just as it does to birth, know, develop, and mature children naturally. This is the nature of a good family. Mature spiritual parents are willing to see developed in the next generation what they never had themselves. They are willing to make sacrifices in order that you might be developed and go further than they could in their own generation.

Jesus lived a life in front of us to show that we would make people uncomfortable even as we healed and restored others to life. He did it in the center of his own Father's affection and affirmation, and so should we. If the life you are living as a Christian is full of caution, playing it safe and careful balance than you may not have a fully surrendered life. You may have a trust issue. What does that look like? It looks like *fear*. Fear of getting it wrong, showing up unprepared, being hurt, failing God and others…all standing in the way of trusting God implicitly. My heart and soul were deeply healed that day as I received my mother and Father's affection and affirmation of me. It made up for all the life events my natural parents were not there for. It set me free to leap when the scent of God's pleasure filled my soul. I want to be an expert at trusting Him because I know where his pleasure is and where he is not.

God is asking us to be filled with his Spirit and to live from the hidden place with him. If you do, I promise you will do radical things for him! God doesn't consult your appearance, your opinion, or even the opinions of others about you. He doesn't even account for your strengths and weaknesses. When he calls you, his confidence is in the calling itself and his design of you. Even before you were placed in your mother's womb according to Jeremiah 1:5, all of God's purpose for you, the purpose he established for you according to his own love for you, exuded from the invisible spirit realm. The only flexible factor in this divine life of calling and purpose is your relationship with

Him and how deeply you are attached to him. He wants your life to be so entrenched in that relational space with him that even when you gain men's approval, you are not moved. I was so moved by what men did not approve of, but I was also delighted when they did approve of me. What a mess that created in a girl who had never been parented or loved well. I needed the affirmation of my heavenly Father. In that delight, I found the joy of obedience.

You are built to move in obedience to your Father. Obedience stems out of a desire to please him, and him alone. I want to lose at the game of popularity! Especially if it means being boldly and passionately in love with the God of the universe! In the following years I had many adventures with God. Even as I write this book, I am sitting amid one of those now. I promise you want that life! It is yours for the taking! This life I am describing of being with God and having a personal heart preference for him is filled with adventures like I described in this chapter. That night, I was just intent on accepting an invitation to preach. I did not expect to get a download of revelation as I looked at a water bottle or experience a personal moment with my own mother.

But what God did was position me with an invitation to *see*. And he made it so compelling, it overpowered my nerves about doing what I was called to do that night, which in turn positioned me to receive an incredible revelation for others. My own freedom to choose to be "with" God in that moment would open a door of understanding for others, as well as allow me to experience a personal moment of parental pride from my mother and God. Those moments changed my life, healed my soul, and opened my passion and calling to other generations at a new level. Sometimes the rubber hits the road of destiny when you choose to follow God into the unknown. This gift of choice is the greatest part of his design for man... and ironically, some would say it is also his downfall, this power of human choice. Let's talk about that next.

Life Application

1. Have you ever had an experience where you saw or heard something you couldn't understand but knew God was in it. Share it with someone. Testify about it.

2. Do you struggle with boldness? Find a verse in your bible that directly confronts that and spend time meditating on it each morning and each night for at least 5 minutes.

3. The author shares a parable from her message that points out how much time we spend on choosing a church, a group, a preacher, an outfit... How did you choose the church that you go to?

4. If you have not chosen a church, what is highlighted from this chapter that might help you make a wise choice?

5. Do you have children, grandchildren or nieces or nephews who are unusual children? Might God have made them that way? How can you encourage their growth and development?

Chapter Seven
FREE TO CHOOSE

He has come to our rescue!

—Romans 7:25

How is it that if we have received the new life with its promise of eternity and Kingdom living with the Father, that we are still so susceptible to sinning? So much of my Christian life was spent trying not to sin and feeling at times like it was a hopeless situation. Remember I defined sin earlier as missing a mark established by God. The more I knew about God and how righteous and holy and pure he was in his intentions, the more I would try to be like him. I identified with Paul when he said in Romans 7 that he felt bound to do the very things he knew he didn't want to do. Yet, even as he declares that the situation seems hopeless, he goes on to give us fresh hope in Romans 7:25. I love François DuToit's translation in The Mirror Translation, "Thank God this is exactly what he has done through Jesus Christ our Leader; he has come to our rescue! I am finally freed from this conflict between the law of my mind and the law of sin in my body." Paul goes on in Romans 8 to then talk with us about how we can live this life of freedom. Romans 8:5 gives us a major key to how Jesus maintained a sinless life while in the body of a man on the Earth. You see Jesus did what Roman's 8:5 says. He set his mind on the realities of the Spirit life - the life that originated from another space or reality where he and his Father had perfect communion. In doing so, his flesh never sinned. Some make the assumption that because according to Philippians 2:5-11, He was a man who had the seed of God inside of him, making Jesus both man and God, that he had no ability to sin. But Hebrews 4:15 tells us the truth. He was a man who was tempted by sin in every way that we are. But he did not sin! He proved that God's original plan for mankind was good. What Adam and Eve could not do, Jesus did! He proved that man was made by God to be sinless. If we set our mind in another place or reality like Jesus, will find the power to not yield to sin. Jesus walked this truth out, even to the cross. 2 Corinthians 5:21 declares, "For He made him who knew no sin *to be* sin for us, that we might become the righteousness of God in him." The divine exchange was our sin - once and for all - for his sinless, right standing with the Father. On the cross of calvary, Jesus took on the issue of sin. The payment for that sin was the sinless man – Jesus. His finished work released us all from the bondage that sin had created for all of mankind throughout time! What an act of history took place then.

When I realized that I had been set free from the curse of sin - truly set free - I began to lose the desire to sin. But this has been a continual process in my life. It happens progressively as I receive revelation from

God about who I really am in light of who Jesus really is. I can't tell you it has happened overnight or that I have yet obtained the fullness of that glorious freedom of choice. I had learned so many ways of comforting myself with sin. If sin is to miss the mark, I felt like a pro at it! Because my body and soul had been so deeply touched by the sin of another, the manners I had developed to feel safe or comforted when stressed or anxious were all physical and emotional. There were seasons where I would try to deal with it through therapy and self-reflective reading. Yet, it was not until I talked about the abuse with a counselor that my affinity for food came to the forefront. It came forward with a black and white picture of a little girl - me - with her arm up to her armpit in a Charles chips can of potato chips. On a visit to see the woman who cared for me at that age, she shared with me that I would have crying jaunts and they could only sooth me by putting me in front of the TV with the can of chips. I would stop crying and even as she was telling me, I could still feel the peace I felt with those chips. The saltiness of the chips was like a stinging astringent that washed away the icky feelings physically and emotionally. Those chips soothed away the uncertainty and discomfort of the sexual abuse. So, at a very early age, I learned how to soothe my emotions with food. Food became my very best friend.

From the age of 14, I suffered from an eating disorder called bulimia. I learned it from a friend. Eat what you want, as much as you want until you are numb, and then in secret away from others, you can purge and get rid of the calories. Until the age of 34, it was one of the biggest secrets of my life. I would sometimes purge up to 10 times a day. At the age of 34, I realized what bondage that comfort was, and I began to fight against it. So much of my life was built upon gaining and losing weight. Dieting, exercising with trainers and friends, fasting, diet drinks and pills were all in my library of self-help habits. I thought of them as ways to undo the destruction that I felt so responsible for.

I built even my sense of freedom on the bondages I had in my life. What I mean by this is that I allowed what I thought freedom looked like to merely be the absence of my bondages and addictions. But the absence of one thing does not mean you automatically possess something better. Each time I found the discipline to stop eating poorly and to start exercising, I would successfully lose weight, but I didn't find the promised joy being slimmer and fitter. Even running two 5K races would not bring me that joy. I merely experienced pride in my accomplishment. But privately, I still felt a blurry void of identity or purpose. Getting slim didn't give me a newfound sense of purpose or value. I was a skinny version of the same girl. I was a mixture of my own dreams in service to the dreams of others. I would grow tired, eat chips again while binge watching TV. I would give up the new habit in favor of feeling safe and settled into someone else's life or calling. The commitments to the ministers and leaders around me were always more compelling than wrestling with what I did not know about myself. My relationships were affected by my inability to be consistent in my own commitments to myself. I was all in or too tired to remember what I promised to do or be.

I lived my life like that old nursery song, "I'm a little teapot, short and stout. Tip me over and pour me out." I thought my life was meant to be a grand act of service to others. As a result, any time I gained strength or fortitude in my body soul or spirit, I would give it away.

I did not recognize the freedom I had was the freedom to choose life and life even more abundantly! John 10:10's promise was like a dangling prize I could not grasp. Listen to me. If you cannot make the decision to value your own life and your freedom of choice enough to steward your body, soul, mind, and time, then you are not fit to give out what you have. Your best offering from this place of lack is merely the folly of poverty. Like someone buying lottery tickets to gain a life they dream of, you give away what you have in the hopes it will change the condition of your own life.

Financial planners will tell you this. If you don't tell your money where to go, your money will tell you where you can and can't go. What you can and can't do. This is absolutely true about the gift of time God has given to you! We have the freedom to choose every day what we do with what we have. But too many times we choose to spend out of guilt, shame or lack. It takes vulnerability and honesty to really assess where you are in your current condition and make a decision to do something about it. Motivation for change comes from one of two places - pain or pleasure. Humanity is filled with the orderly voice of discipline and pain. We go to the gym out of a sense of beating our bodies back into submission. We starve ourselves or add the discipline of a diet to beat our appetites back into a place to support our weight goal. We go without so our children can have what they need. This is all carefully packed in wrappings that promise you will feel great when you do this. What happens when you don't? Do you really understand what it means when Galatians 5:1 declares that it was for an existence of freedom that we have been set free by Jesus? What type of freedom is this? I am discovering this in a fresh way every day! It is the freedom of choice!

I began to master the condition of my body, soul and mind when I discovered the true freedom of the power of choice. I can choose to live right now in the midst of God's delight and joy for me. Choice is a powerful thing. We make a big deal about freedom in my country – the United States of America. We elevate freedom itself to the status of idolatry! Yet freedom is not freedom without the understanding of choice. To be truly free is to *choose* what you *desire to do*, not just what you *don't want to do*.

The Mosaic law of the Old Testament gave us a glimpse of what we would be able to do positionally were we to live from the heart of God. Yet, the law was a harsh master as Galatians 3:24 declares. It only proved what we could not do in our own flesh. We could not achieve true freedom through it. The law held us responsible for our sin. We needed Jesus to set us free from sin and the requirements of the law, but more so, we needed the same seed that he bore within Him, to be *IN* us! The Passion Translation of this verse declares, "The law becomes a gateway to lead us to the Messiah so that we would be saved by faith." By this acceptance of the work of Jesus the Messiah or

Deliverer, we can live by faith in the realm of God - the Father of lights and perfection (James 1:17)! We no longer need to use our liberty in Christ to fight a war in our flesh or mind against sin. A life cultivated in the knowledge of the love of God for us, the life of the Spirit in us and the mind of Christ about us is the place where freedom rules and reigns. Light and perfection is a reference to truth, clarity, peace, purpose, love and right living. How? In the land of choice...

This other place of freedom is revealed in this passage:

> **For as many of you as were baptized into Christ have put on Christ.**
>
> **—Galatians 3:27**

Being baptized as this passage speaks of is to be fully immersed in something.[10] It is not meant to be the submersion of our bodies in the baptism tank at church that changes us. That is a symbolic act, demonstrating our change. True baptism is to become fully saturated in all your being and clothed by the reality of Christ in us and through us, until we become completely and radically God's sons and daughters! We are heirs of everything that is his. If Jesus has access to it according to the Father's desire, then so do we! The question then becomes one of relationship only. If we have need of anything, but do not have what he has promised, we have not yet realized it in our mind. Our spirit knows it. Our flesh desires it. But our mind is often still captured by the old thoughts and habits of life. Keep in mind that the culture around us champions that natural way of living in response to people, places, and things as the "real life." But it is not real. It is fading and passing away even as I write, and you read.

The only lasting life that we can hope to spend our freedom on is the one we are living now from the realm of the Spirit as a child of God. If you want real results that remain with you for eternity and then you need to learn to yield to the intrinsic and invisible realm of faith. That is the challenge. Faith in Jesus is essential to understanding the love of the Father for all of us! The activation of the first seed of Christ in Jesus was the goal of the Father's work on the cross. ***We are not mere humans trapped in a cosmic prison of revolving temptation!*** We are sons and daughters of God and built to prove, just as Jesus did, the value and indestructible nature of the divine DNA, regardless of the threat of sin. We eat the reward of an abundant life by partaking of the divine nature of life now inside of us, a new nature that frees us from the desire for sin and death. Abundance or life everlasting is the byproduct of a sinless life. Everything God has created is meant to lean towards you with natural reward as a son or daughter of God. We are called to live in a world seemingly captured by sin and *not* become engrossed with defeating sin. Instead, filled with the power of God we fight evil on behalf of the Kingdom of God. We demonstrate life-giving hope, with God's love, and acceptance. This is our true mission.

We have been guilty of one thing as Christians. We often have more faith in the power of sin than we do in the power of our new nature in God. Our new nature that is growing into a tree of life is designed to hit the mark every time! We have an amazing architect for a Father. We need a mind renewal. We must learn to live from the place where that old mind and its thoughts begin to submit to our new nature that desires to choose life, not death, every time! I am developing a new set of habits in my mind that are supported by this truth: I meditate on the fact that I am not given to sin. To choose sin is to choose death. Sin and death are the antithesis of my Father and my spiritual family. Why would an eternal being subject themselves again to death? I am now given to the life of the Spirit and the ways of right living that Jesus was, and still is. In Isaiah 11, Jesus' lifestyle was foretold by Isaiah. He will not determine a thing, event or a person by his natural ears and eyes. He won't be an echo of the Earth! But the Spirit of God in Him - the spirit of wisdom, understanding, counsel, might, knowledge and of the fear of the Lord - shall lead him from a place of delight. Every judgement, decision, and encounter would be determined by that lifestyle. I want to experience that in my life! I believe you do, too.

In every season of my life as I press into God, I find freedom from another habit birthed out of the sins of my past. One of the most difficult for me to surrender was that eating disorder. But through a series of events, through counseling and times of prayer with the Lord, I was able to come to terms with what had happened to me, forgiving and releasing myself from the prison of self-hatred. The cycle of binging and purging was broken for me then.

However, the habit of comforting with food stayed with me. It was the way I created safety in my broken self-care system. I could control it. I didn't purge, I maintained a handle on the habit, but it often handled me back! It had a voice that whispered lies to me. I wondered at times if I needed deliverance ministry. I would diet, lose weight and then begin to hear the beckoning of that familiar tone reminding me how easy it was to purge to get rid of weight. Every diet would eventually open a door to that familiar voice in my mind. I needed help that only the Lord could give me. It came to me through revelation of the word of God and understanding.

I appeal to you therefore, brethren, and beg of you in view of [all] the mercies of God, to make a decisive dedication of your bodies [presenting all your members and faculties] as a living sacrifice, holy (devoted, consecrated) and well pleasing to God, which is your reasonable (rational, intelligent) service and spiritual worship. Do not be conformed to this world (this age), [fashioned after and adapted to its external, superficial customs], but be transformed (changed) by the [entire] renewal of your mind [by its new ideals and its new attitude], so that you may prove [for yourselves] what is the good and acceptable and perfect will of God, even the thing which is good and acceptable and perfect [in His sight for you].

—Romans 12:1-2 (AMP)

The Lord showed me that I was beautiful and that my body was a temple to be honored and cared for, and I surrendered my rights and privileges for the care of that temple to Holy Spirit. I realized that I had a joyful relationship in the inner spaces of my heart and soul with the Lord. I loved having him occupy that space with me in real and tangible ways. But I had retained the rights to the container - my physical body - and all the care and attention it needed. I falsely believed that this body was given to sin and temptation. I didn't know it could join me in that place of love and affection inside of me. My love/hate relationship was not with food; it was with my temple. I hated my body. Not only did I have a faulty alarm system for my temple, but it also had all kinds of inclinations toward destructive substances that did not help it. In fact, I later found that many things I had been eating I was allergic to! My self-hatred of my body had to submit to my self-love. God had shown and revealed to me that he loved me and how amazing I was to him. Now, I needed to use my freedom of choice to love myself completely.

The thoughts of my mind did need to change. Not in a disciplinary way, but a relational way. Once I got a revelation of Father's love and intention for me, I could trust him with an area of my life that I thought I should manage and get right for him. My shame became relief! I lost my curiosity for the next diet, the obsession with my body, the need to eat to comfort and exchanged it for the "yoke of the Lord". (Matthew 11:30) The anointing of God is not just for others; it is for you, too! The yoke that is easy, is the one that is smeared with the anointing of God's power to do the impossible, is first for you! The overflow or the anointing that comes upon you for a purpose is for others.

I love the story of Elisha being called into the prophet's ministry in 1 Kings 19. He accepts Elijah's invitation to follow him by burning His old yokes and feeding his oxen to his community. In following the invitation for more, he left all possible ways of satisfying himself in his old life behind him.

The life of abundance that God calls his children into can only be fully realized that way. I had to let go of the hard-handed way I dealt with my flesh and accept the light and easy ways of the spirit-led life. What did that look like? I didn't lose my love of food, but it fell into a much more appropriate place in my life. I still love to eat. I consider myself a "foodie", but I don't love it more than I love him. I don't love it more than I love myself. I am aware of its potential to harm me if misused. I have also found that anything I can do without him might not be worth doing. Binge watching TV series required eating a bag of chips for me. So, I might not want to give myself away to that idolatry. What is idolatry? It is the worship of anything else that requires you to turn from God to worship it. It is to use the tremendous freedom of choice to give yourself away to something that has a sense of promise to it but is potentially harmful to you.

I want you to take a moment to think about how you might be living out an area of life separate from God. Yes, I know he is there always. Yes, nothing can separate us from him, and his abiding love for us. But we do separate ourselves from him in pockets of our lives to do things that satisfy an old itch. You are a new creation with the Christ-life inside of you and as 2 Corinthians 5:17 declares the old is dead and gone, completely having been removed from you by God. Yet your mind may still reference it as memories. It is an easy catalogue to go to. But the adventure of discovery is worth it! We have the power through God's grace to create new memories and relationships with food, people, activities, and hobbies that empower us to be who we truly are. We are free of the stain of sin and all of its habitual rhythms attached to self-care, when we surrender all we are to God and allow him to define us.

How did I discover this and finally surrender in that area of my life? I read Psalm 23:4 in the Passion Translation which declares that by the "waters of reflection my soul remembers who I am." I discovered as I gazed into God's heart and mind for me that I was not a food addict, addicted to self-pleasure and gratification. I was a daughter of God who like Queen Esther had been prepared for a special life with a mission like no other. I could not choose food in place of that discovery anymore. It just lost its compelling influence to drive my life. And I was left with an understanding and appreciation for the goodness of fruit and vegetables, fine wine and cheeses, herbs, and delicate choice pieces of meat. I enjoy them with him. He was invited to *my* feasting table, and I was changed forever!

What area of your life do you need to surrender to God and receive power from the inner place of relationship and revelation? Perhaps you feel God calling to you. Have you left behind everything of the old life and habits that helped you take care of yourself on your own? If you don't understand the value of the relationship to which you have been called with God in this amazing Kingdom life, you may not know you are acting in ways that reek of poverty, rather than abundance. This unique place of peace and oneness is such a place of power. It means that wherever you show up, He is there with you and whatever you are facing, he is facing too! Much of my life I was so busy wanting what I didn't have that I couldn't see what I already had available to me. I had a foundational resting place of security, affirmation, and love in God's family. Yet I traveled like a transient vagabond in the fields of his grace. I needed to come and build a nest in the reality of family. I want to dive into the reality of this Kingdom family life with you. This is truly the best part of the story!

Life Application

1. What area of your life remains separate from God, held onto as if the old you still exist, and needs it?

2. What revelation or relational truth do you need to experience to let go and let God into that area?

3. The yoke of God is easy because of the anointing of his spirit upon you. Give an example of what the yoke that is easy has made possible for you. Be specific.

4. Self-sufficiency is idol worship! What area or habit are you holding onto – maybe even tell yourself that when it is right you will win God's approval?

5. Pray a prayer of dedication according to Romans 12:1. Ask God to forgive you and to help you release that to him. Bow your head and ask him to put the yoke that is easy upon you. Let it bind you to his anointing. Let it change the way you approach that old area.

Chapter Eight
THE PRIVILEGES OF FAMILY

Then Jesus answered and said to them, "Most assuredly, I say to you, the Son can do nothing of Himself, but what He sees the Father do; for whatever He does, the Son also does in like manner.

—John 5:19

As I embraced the truth of my relationship with the Father through the work of my brother Jesus, I have found a place of peace and purpose that is sustainable. Peace is only found in embracing a life in him. I work hard at becoming myopic about the process. Myopia is also known as nearsightedness or to be shortsighted. It is to be able to only see what is directly in front of you while being blissfully unable to see what is visible in the distance. It is to be - to just be - in the day you are in, fully present.

Don't get me wrong, I love to see ahead! But knowing what is ahead comes with a temptation to try to control outcomes in advance. Now, I accept that the adventure of seeing what God sees is only possible if I allow God to be my focus. I embrace what I don't know yet as an adventure, remembering that God goes before me and will share with me what I need to know when I need to know about it. There is a place of rest and purpose in God that lifts you above even the most difficult of circumstances in life. We don't talk about that place enough. I want to sing about it and live a life from it. To champion its peace, power and purpose because it is the only way to lasting change.

So often we Christians look like half dead salmon who are struggling against a river to return home to die. I have met so many of God's children who just felt weary to me in their souls, jaded in their minds and hurt in their hearts. They just keep pushing uphill, waiting for the glory of God to come in the next wave of revival, the next anointed something. I remember seeing salmon like this in a visit to Washington State. They were huge and lumbering slowly against the current. They often took a rest in a pool and then would try again to swim against the pull of the water. They had enormous grey chunks of broken flesh gouged out of their sides from all the sharp edges they had encountered along the way. I couldn't imagine how far they had come and who they had encountered. I wondered how they would make it home. I asked my host, "How is it that they make it home!?" She replied, "Many do not but the homing signal in their DNA demands that they return to the home where they were birthed from."

I have met many Christians who resemble those salmon, who are living just to die. I never want to dishonor the fact that clearly, we are going to face trials, losses, and betrayals in life. Yet, what appeal is there to this Kingdom if we just live to die and escape this world? We are called to live bravely and fiercely so that others might be inspired by our lives. To develop a sense of tribe and family amongst those who love God with such a messy beauty that it undoes our fears and dispels our shame.

God had a dream that we would discover ourselves within the construct of families that champion this kingdom mindset around us. He said in Psalm 68:6 that he places the lonely, solitary person inside of family. That is his promise to us! Yet for so many there is no family, connection, community, and support for the process of life. There are many reasons, and some are legitimate. You may have every reason to not trust, but I want to say to you that you need others around you to really heal from the inside out. Even those salmon swam upstream together, limping along and leaning on each other in shallow pools together. The hurts you choose to carry with you in this life will disable, disarm, and destroy you. Your enemy will do everything to use your hidden wounds to end your life by separating you from God's love, your own being, and the rest of God's family. You may even leave this life with your cup still half full of purpose. I want to die empty!

> *Therefore, since we are justified (acquitted, declared righteous, and given a right standing with God) through faith, let us [grasp the fact that we] have [the peace of reconciliation to hold and to enjoy peace with God through our Lord Jesus Christ (the Messiah, the Anointed One).*
>
> **—Romans 5:1** (AMP)

There is a place of rest and peace that can access joy even in the worst of circumstances. Without this place established in our life, our peace will be dependent upon our circumstances. Rather, God wants our circumstances to bow to our peace and the collective peace and power of those who surround us in community. Jesus stood up in a fishing boat with his disciples trembling in fear around him at the storm intent on killing them. The storm had a purpose, to keep them from encountering and delivering the demoniac on the other side of the lake. Jesus didn't deal with the storm to address the circumstances of those that he was surrounded by in that moment. His focus was not so future-focused on the ministry on the other side of the lake that he could not hear the fear in the ones he was with at that moment. He heard their fear. He acknowledged it. And he made the storm submit to his compassion and peace. I daresay he went back to sleep then. I wonder if the disciples did, too? Sometimes what you can't face alone can be changed entirely by those who surround you. But you have to let them see your fear, pain and questions. God does not draw back from our fear. He doesn't respond because of it, either. He responds to faith, to someone with faith to access his heart and purpose and say something different about what is happening. We have the right to access truth and exalt it above the facts we know.

According to Romans 5:1, we have been given access to the very heart of God. Regardless of our perfections or imperfections, Jesus made a way for us to come. He reconciled every sin with his own blood.

We have been reconciled to our true family of origin! Francois DuToit says it this way in the Mirror Translation's footnotes on this verse, *"This gives context to faith and finds expression in unhindered, face to face friendship with God! Jesus Christ is the head of this union."*[11] That simply means that Jesus himself was the first one to step into this family union of unbroken fellowship with the Father. In the same way pioneers are the first to go into a land and create a path so that others might take the same route, Jesus was the first to take up that relational space of sonship. But we are invited into that space of relationship, too. I love that Francois says it is a "face to face" place of access. In that face-to-face place with God according to Galatians 5:6, this love encounter activates our faith and gives it the power to take action. Every other application of faith life is a formula that takes time to apply. The Word of Faith movement birthed in the late 1900s was powerful. They taught us to apply our faith to the words that we speak and thereby cause those words to come about. "Just like Jesus did," they touted. But the issue became clear over time that sometimes the words of our soul can take form and with "faith" attached to them, they manifested airplanes, cars, and mansions for many of the fathers of this faith. I have great respect for those leaders. I was birthed out of the ministry of a great man of God who taught me some of the same principles. Not all of them were flawed, but a few did not have that ***relational context of revelation*** that causes us to pursue what enriches God's kingdom beyond personal gain.

What I discovered in the Word of God is that the God kind of faith always comes hand in hand with love. There is an unparalleled kind of fruit produced when faith is activated by love. Galatians 5:6 declares that faith finds it expression or work only by the way of love. So, what was that other faith I pondered? I believe it was merely the authority of men made in the image of God manifesting through their authority and faith, the works of their soul. Belief is always meant to be accompanied by love, and the love of God in us. In John 11:40 and Mark 9:23, two of the most quoted scriptures about faith, the belief that moves and changes things is in correlation to seeing and knowing what God knows. Even Jesus only did what his father desired.

> *Then Jesus answered and said to them, "Most assuredly, I say to you, the Son can do nothing of Himself, but what He sees the Father do; for whatever He does, the Son also does in like manner.*

> **—John 5:19**

We are the sons and daughters of God that Romans 8 declares that the Earth is crying out for the releasing of. Why is the Earth crying out for our releasing and what are we being released from? There is a simple way of life that is powerful and clear and accurate. It is not an uncertain sound, diluted by the decision-making models of the world itself. It is a life of freedom. Freedom to choose to live in the center of our Father's delight. Jesus clearly said in John 5:19 that he could not do anything apart from the Father. In fact, he said he needed to see what the Father was doing first in order to copy it. "Like manner" is to do something as closely to the original source as possible. Not exactly the same but from the same heart and model of purpose. How did he get this type of clarity? He stayed with his Father in both private and public life. He built a life in private spaces that was so rich that he could still attain his Father's will despite the cries and needs of others. Did you know Jesus did not minister blindly to every single person he met who had a need? He didn't take the liberty to assume he knew what the Father's heart was for the blind man, or the rich man. Today we have formulas for evangelism, models for healing, recipes for business success. Many are birthed out of God's heart. They are not faulty. Yet they are only meant to be tools in the hands of spirit-led sons and daughters who are obedient to their Father's will as they seek to genuinely know people by God's spirit.

Hebrews 4:9-11 asks us to be zealous to exertion, passionate to enter God's rest. For his rest is the only place where our own desires can submit to his peace and purpose. There we can be closest to his heart and get the most accurate read on our own heart's leading.

Jesus said this powerful statement to his disciples. "The poor you will have with you always. But you will not always have me." (Matthew 26:11) Here the disciples were in a pivotal moment of history where a woman whose life had been deeply rescued by Jesus was in the habit of taking him at his word. She believed his predicated story of his pending death. This woman was once a prostitute but had become a follower of Jesus. Her heart preference was for him and so a fallen, yet also forgiven woman had grasped the truth of what Jesus had been saying. He was leaving to die a terrible death soon. In the sense of being void of his physical absence, she paid him the highest tribute by giving her all at that moment. Her precious, costly bottle of oil was laced with revealed truth. She anointed Jesus for his pending burial.

More so, she became the first to recognize the value of his death. What he had done for her in rescuing her from her fallen life, he was going to do for everyone. The disciples on the other hand were thinking only of the cost of feeding the crowds they believed they would see for the next few weeks. They saw her sacrifice as financially detrimental to the crowds that would gather to see the Messiah. You see, without being rooted in the spirit realm where God exists without interference, we can be lost in the minutia of outside noise and opinions. Without him as our place of reality, we will prioritize every expense of time, money and effort based on its Earthly value. Or we can be like this woman and recognize the value of God's will above the demands of others, even our own flesh and soul. Her tears were an outpouring of the knowledge that she would lose Jesus to death. Yet she agreed with his will and anointed him for his burial.

This awareness and lifestyle of always leaning towards God in our hearts and mind can seem confining to everyday life. It is not. It can liberate you from doing what everyone else is doing to have an impact. It liberates you from religious duty to please God, into a life of clarity and purpose within a family line that is generational and global. It can keep us from investing too deeply with our humanity into the human condition for the sake of having a life of deep spiritual impact on the conditions of the world around us. I dare say that without the comfort of this confinement to the Father's will alone, we will never experience peace on the Earth. God's will is peace, but the need is too overwhelming for one individual, ministry, company or generation. Jesus said to his disciples that the poor of the Earth will be with us. He alone has the strategies to reach them. Too many ministers and leaders of nonprofit organizations have burned out trying to do more than they truly can in their own humanity. The needs of those struck by poverty itself is so great that they bowed to it and allowed the desire to meet that need become a form of idolatry. This type of idolatry is cruel even when led by compassion. It is a harsh taskmaster, extracting much, giving little back, and yet it is never enough to truly stamp out the nature of the disease of sin and all its evil effects on mankind. The designer of the universe has strategies that will require leaders to partner their influence in a way that many are involved in the solution, not just a few. But to gain these strategies we must develop a relationship with the God who does life face-to-face every day and gain a family perspective. God knows best how to solve the hard things, and he is willing to share those solutions within his family. Like that woman, our influence like hers will far exceed our capacity, and our testimony will far surpass our own generation.

For almost 20 years of my life, I was deeply entrenched in a local church with a desire to impact the world for change. I shared with you that in my own brokenness, I falsely believed that if I could fix the condition of other people's lives. I would feel valued and of service to the Kingdom. I even believed that this is what God expected of me and so I gave my life freely and deeply to the vision of others. Even when they often failed to finish what they started, I would continue to pray over it and over them that there would be a change that would cause what they were building to be completed. I didn't just ask, I poured out my life, prayers and money to support this happening. Though we accomplished many great things, there were many we did not finish. I counted the failure to finish as a failure to God and it was deeply personal to me. I felt that failure. I felt like a failure. So, I would try harder. My life was a cycle of intensely hard workdays, long days at times managing construction or design projects.

These seasons would be followed by an intense fatigue that would come over me and drag me down like a victim in the ocean accosted by the will of its waves. I would fight against its pull, but it was compelling and eventually I would get physically sick, emotionally depressed, and eventually was diagnosed with an autoimmune disorder. Even after taking the latest medications for this disorder, the doctors were befuddled by my lack of response. They explained to me that I was experiencing "breakthrough activity," which merely meant that despite the powerful drugs they were feeding me, my body was still pushing through the effect of the drugs almost as if they were candy rather than the latest biologic agents. There are wounds that never show on the body but are deeper and more hurtful than anything that bleeds visibly. What you do about those hidden places will either find ways to slowly kill you or bring you healing and make you stronger. And they do not buff out with kingdom work or Christian duty.

The doctors asked me what I did for a living. Imagine my embarrassment in having to tell them I was a support pastor and on staff at a large church locally. One doctor said, "Are you sure that is what you are supposed to be doing with your life? Because it seems to be killing your body." I laughed it off. I could not hear those words with comfort and clarity. I was too busy working for Jesus and finishing the work of the kingdom before I left the Earth. I was pushing forward like those half-dead salmon swimming upstream, furthering the work of God through the lives of the men and women I followed. Two years into the disease process, I was told I would be in a wheelchair and completely disabled by pain and deformity if I did not find a way to help my body respond to the meds. At the same time, I broke out with an infection that required me to take a drug holiday from all meds to allow my antibiotics to work. The decision to "holiday" from life was seemingly forced upon me. It was suggested with a firm tone that I take time off from my job and allow my body to rest and fight what was happening to it. I had to listen.

I took a six-week sabbatical from work in ministry. During the first two weeks of the sabbatical, I was a mess. I felt guilty, rejected, set up and put down. I couldn't stop thinking about all the hanging ends at work and if I had covered all the people and systems adequately. After two weeks the Lord required me to go away. I will never forget the first day that the next stage of my reset started. I had gone to bed knowing where I would drive to in the morning. It was a small beach type town on Lake Ontario. I packed a bag with my journal, pens, bible and iPod to listen to worship. I was going to go find God, for me.

When I woke in the morning it was raining! Pouring cats and dogs. He said go, so I went anyways. Literally the moment I passed the sign bearing the name of the small town, the rain stopped. The drenching downpour dried up. A restaurant there opened their patio over the water for me and dried off the table and chairs for me to sit at. The waitress served me lunch and hot tea for 4 hours while I listen to the sound of my discomfort and submitted it to God in writing. He stilled me and began speaking to me of his abiding love for me. He did not see me as a workhorse. I was his daughter in need of his love. The hot tea reminded me of one thing I do remember my Irish father doing for me when I was sick. He would make toast and sweet milky hot Lipton tea for us to dunk it in when we were sick. It was a cure all for him. Probably from his own mother.

I was comforted that day by Father God and unknown to me then, I began to rediscover some beautiful things about my father through that cup of hot Irish tea. The next four weeks I rested and adjusted my diet and exercise. Sometimes I would sleep for hours during the daytime. I would curl up in a blanket on the couch and feel like I was wrapped in Poppa God's love for me.

He cherished me and wanted to heal me. He destroyed the power of the words spoken over me that would try to destroy my life by disabling my body. I would not be in a wheelchair. I would not lose my purpose to sickness. He began to speak to me of cherishing me and my spirit was strengthened, and my design made clearer to me.

If you have been in this season of burnout in the past or perhaps find yourself in it now, the only way of escape is to find the solitude and quiet calm of Father God's heart for you. My season of burnout in ministry took 6 weeks of my life to reset to peace. it cost me relationships and I committed professional suicide to get the rest my soul and body were begging for. I walked on piers by the water and sat for hours with the Lord in the sunlight. I cried myself to sleep at night and woke with a dull headache from the demanding dreams I had at night. My soul processed its pain and fear in the night season because I could not speak of them in the day light.

Until I spent time letting go of what was sustaining the pace of my life, the demand and din of voices around me, I could not find him as my sole provider of peace. I merely allowed him to share my life. I causally talked to him about my challenges on the go. He got to walk and talk with me or sit down and shut up. I know that sounds callous and it should. It was how I treated my Father. I had to become more zealous for God than I had been for the mission I was accomplishing for him. I discovered he is not a harsh task master. He does not ask me to sacrifice myself for ministry. He already completed that sacrifice. He taught me to find the gentle rhythms of grace that Jesus spoke of in Matthew 11.

Are you tired? Worn out? Burned out on religion? Come to me. Get away with me and you'll recover your life. I'll show you how to take a real rest. Walk with me and work with me—watch how I do it. Learn the unforced rhythms of grace. I won't lay anything heavy or ill-fitting on you. Keep company with me and you'll learn to live freely and lightly.

—Matthew 11:28-30 (MSG)

This recovery of my life was essential to my restoration to ministry and to my own calling. I pray that if you are struggling in this weariness yourself, that you would have the courage to say no. Leave room for the rest of the family of God to work with him to meet the needs of people. To say yes to yourself and the call for God's peace from deep inside of you can feel selfish but it is a matter of honor. We honor our own design when we recognize that what we are being asked to do is not in line with our design and purpose. Moreover, it is a matter of honor when we take the time for everyone to be engaged in what we are about corporately. There is a place for everyone to do their part. Yes, it does take more time then. I have been guilty of doing way more than I needed to because the results were faster in my eyes. And of course, more controllable. But when you choose to see every plan of God through the lens of family, you will be more aware of the "who" in a project, then the "how" or "when."

Have you ever played a board game with more than four players? It is cumbersome, slow, and not easy to control the outcomes. But the fun and the antics that take place in those moments with that many people are what build a family or circle of friends. It draws us closer as we celebrate the "who" rather than worry about time and cost. I have found that God will cover the time and cost when we focus on "who is supposed to do this with me."

If you are under a weight of responsibility that is bigger than you or have isolated yourself by only doing what you can control, there is a way out, but it may include the gift of rest and reset with God. We are all moored to him in our depths, but you may have to cut some lines, ties, and commitments to find that mooring again. I pray you find the fortitude to take the time to retire with him for a season and let him teach you the unforced rhythms of grace. It is there you will discover the free and light life meant to be so compelling to the world. It is there you will discover your Father and big brother Jesus in such a way that you begin to understand the family relationship that is the essence of his purpose for mankind. Though men and women of God may fail to understand their role in your life in light of this lens of family, He never will.

This family mindset is not about doing birthday parties together every year with your church family and friends. It's about a way of honor and commitment that does not see another person as a means to an end. They are the means. They are the end. This is God's lens towards us. He gave his own first-born son to ensure we could have this privilege. Jesus is the first of the best of us. But he is not meant to be the last. We can learn a lot from his life here on the Earth, especially because his example does not include the weight of the sin and selfish motivation. One of the first things that Jesus did when entering into ministry was gather a circle around him. They were not perfect! But they were chosen to help him be who he was called to be and do what he was called to do. Ultimately there was one mission he had to accomplish alone with his Father, but all other work he did with 3 or 12 or 70, or more.

The privilege of family is doing life with God, not for him. Together as one, we can accomplish so much more with so much more ease. This book is being written and published in an era of time that is uniquely positioning the body of Christ to tap into God's mind about community or tribe. He wants to teach us how to experience the life of Christ personally in those who live a continent away from us. For centuries we have limited our gathering together to the size of a building. But there are breakthroughs coming in technology that will no longer bind us to impersonal conversations device to device. Quantum technology will allow us to experience each other personally, even from afar. I pray that the Kingdom of God would harness this and create expansive networks of relational conversations with people of like interests. I pray we are forerunners, not catching up to the world, as we often have been. There are privileges to God's purpose for family that we cannot grasp on our own. Our knowledge is too often based on personal experience or opinions from others. Our wisdom can come from scholars, scientists and the renowned writers of the Earth. But there is something special that happens when you get understanding by experience. My own awful experiences with my father were replaced and healed through an experience with a cup of Irish tea enjoyed with my true father – God.

To gain the depths of the privilege and purpose of family, we need to look at it much more deeply than we have. To do so I want to help you grasp the difference between getting knowledge, gaining wisdom, and living from the experience of understanding according to scripture. God said so many things to us and continues to, that are not meant to just be memorized or memorialized. They are meant to be experienced and lived out through the experience with others. Family is so much more than we have realized. God's DNA in us is magnetizing, drawing us all together as an expression of the bride of Jesus Christ!

Life Application

1. In one sentence describe your experience of family growing up.

2. Was that sentence in any way different than the author describes God's heart for family? How?

3. Have you discovered family in your life that mirrors and echoes God back to you?

4. Has your family, natural or spiritual, ever contributed to overwhelm or burnout in your life?

5. How can you address burnout if you are experiencing it? Pray and ask God to get a strategy to balance your life out. This means time for God, time for you, time for your family and then everyone else must see if there is room for them. Be honest and ask a friend for help with this. God wants to help you through community.

Chapter Nine
LADY WISDOM COMES CALLING

Whatever it takes to gain Wisdom, do it.

To gain understanding, do it! Never forget this!

Never stray from what I am telling you.

If you don't forsake Lady Wisdom, she will protect you.

Love her, and she will faithfully take care of you.

Gaining sound judgment is key, so first things first: go after Lady Wisdom! Now, whatever else you do, follow through to understanding.

Cherish her, and she will help you rise above the confusion of life, your possibilities will open up before you.

Embrace her, and she will raise you to a place of honor in return.

She will provide the finishing touch to your character—grace; she will give you an elegant confidence.

—Proverbs 4:5-9 (VOICE)

Henry Matisse said that to look at something as if we had not seen it before requires great courage.[12] I have found in my life, and I think it is true for too much of humanity, that we are content to know a little bit about a lot of things. Because I was so often alone in my life, I struggled desperately to get the knowledge to make really good decisions. I hoped to avoid failure by knowing how to do everything, right. When I became a Christian, there was such a wealth of information being taught that I became even more endeared to the very idea of knowledge itself. But I was so enamored with knowledge, I found myself overlooking the opportunities I had to find the gifts of understanding simply by noticing what was highlighted in my spirit consistently. There are key topics that would come up in my life or be highlighted to me regularly. I had a choice. They could be easily overlooked, or I could pause and talk to God about them. One of those things was the topic of community. I have always been curious about the human need for belonging. Perhaps it was birthed out of the sense of never fitting in throughout my life. I sometimes ponder whether that is part of God's redemptive plan in my life. He allowed me to be formed in a family and culture where I always felt rejection, like I was a square peg being jammed into a round hole. Belonging for me was not just a need, it was a mission.

Even after I began to release forgiveness and experience healing and restoration of my original design, the desire to understand the dynamics of belonging continued to create a curiosity in me. In churches we form fellowships, serving teams, evening suppers, women's ministries, men's ministries…the lists can be endless here. In society we form honor societies, secret societies, social clubs, and so many others. I have found that for the most part these tend to be meant to celebrate a similar viewpoint for a general body of people. It is rare for a group of people to associate out of a desire to discover the unknown. If course medical or science researchers pursue them. Yet the Church as a collective have a habit of gathering to glean from the discovery of the gospel already revealed. There is so much more available!

There is an amazing church in Nashville, Tennessee that was formed out of a small group of people who joined a young couple who felt God sent them from Australia to Nashville to "cleanse the waters." They were worshippers and so they started with who they were. A handful of people joined them in that place of just worshipping in the basement of their home. I have had the privilege of meeting a few of those people whose lives were changed by the invitation to "come and do what we do, with us." The thread I have found in the story of the growth of this church is that its focus on worshipping together created a space for them to hear from God individually and corporately. They equated this feeling of finding a fit in the nest of God's love and acceptance as gaining a sense of belonging. Their worship is amazing and intimate. But more so is the story of their roots.

The incredible picture of a few people nestling close to God for the mere joy of not just finding his pleasure but experiencing it in and through each other. Ultimately, we are made for connection. In God's family when we connect with someone else, we are multiplied, not just added to. That connection with God's heart, message and gifts or aptitudes within them brings forth a holistic message of family that enriches everyone in the room. Beyond our own capacity to connect with him, we are enriched through others. As Paul said in Colossians 1:12, we are enriched as we come into the knowledge of the inheritance of God's love and light which is spread abroad in all God's children yet face to face with us now.

You see wisdom is a communal offering. And it is meant to be pursued beyond her initial offerings. The passage in Proverbs 4 goes so far as to say that if you don't forsake what you gained (wisdom), what you know will protect you in the future. Lady wisdom, as Proverbs refers to wisdom, will give you the tools you need to make good decisions. Yet, I believe it is only in pursuing understanding that we get to make "God" decisions, for understanding elevates you up above what has already been visibly set into motion on the Earth. What do I mean by God decisions? It is to decide based on what has not yet been seen, but has become *known*, by you. It is to stake your life on the invisible because you have come to *understand what is not visible* and how it intends to interact with the visible realm.

Understanding will expose you to a level of thought and imagination that causes what seems impossible to be filled with endless possibilities of actualization. Furthermore, if you follow her faithfully, she will lead you into the land of pioneers where men and women are celebrated for their new inventions, ideas, strategies, and ingenuity. Understanding allows you to properly place yourself in the right position, at the right time, with the right strategy and tools for what is at hand to be used *for that which was formerly hidden from view.* There is a grace and style to showing up during chaos with truly life-giving seeds to change the course of history.

I fear that in our information dense technological advances, we have opened the door to knowledge and wisdom but failed to pursue understanding. As a result, we now face a variety of cultural problems, and often we feel incapable of addressing them with strategies that bring real lasting change. We have settled for band-aid treatments when God is offering us the opportunity to heal the culture around us and build new stability for the generations that will follow us. The Church appears to be more endeared to saving souls like a catch and release fishing program than effecting lasting Kingdom influence. We lead people in the sinner's prayer and release them back into their messy lives with the promise that one day everything will be better when they die and get to the other side. Rather than being culture changers and Kingdom influencers, we rubber stamp people with a promise that they will be changed one day. We forsake the privilege of seeing them transformed by getting to know them and doing life with them. It does such an injustice to the gospel message. The few churches that have taken the discipleship mandate seriously have done so with a heavy-handed eye on education. How many of you know that if classroom education alone could change a person, we would be so much better off in the world! We are a mixed society. Some are well-educated professional students who have done nothing with what they learned. Others are those who have only learned from the experiences of others around them and are mimicking their mistakes out of a belief they can't do better than those before them. It can send a huge ripple in culture when someone, educated or not, gets curious enough to ask God for more. If he is an author, and a finisher of the story, and there is still a story taking place, might he not have more to say? So many times I have had questions but when I asked them, I was challenged to consider why I was not content with what I had already been told. So I started to go to God with those questions. I searched dictionaries, commentaries, interlinear translations, until I had a light bulb moment that connected thoughts for me. If it was something I did not know previously, I would ask God to show me an example of it in the Bible and he would! Now if I see something I don't think is clear, I say something to God about it. I ask him what his thoughts are about it. I have discovered he loves to talk and teach me. I find so much peace when those moments happen!

The key to true lasting change is to learn the art of gaining understanding. I love how the Passion Translation of Proverbs 4:8-9 declares how she (understanding) will give you the gift of elegant confidence called grace:

> **Cherish her, and she will help you rise above the confusion of life, your possibilities will open up before you.**

Embrace her, and she will raise you to a place of honor in return.

She will provide the finishing touch to your character—grace; she will give you an elegant confidence.

I have always had a drive to understand. I could never settle for getting someone else's opinion or doctrine on a topic. Long after others stopped asking questions, I have always pushed to know more. If I couldn't get an answer, I would put my question on a shelf. That shelf was not my own, but one that God and I had a deal about. If I put it on that particular shelf, he would answer it when he was ready. This generally means, *when I am ready* for that level of understanding. I have been amazed through the years how often something has fallen off that shelf into my view with the answer attached. God honors curiosity because it indicates a level of relationship that has faith in his goodness and faithful nature to answer. The encounters I share with you that I have had with Jesus, have been difficult to recount to others. They transcend the natural realm. I find myself trying to explain "into" people something that was so real I can still vividly recall the experience as if it were yesterday. Wisdom is meant to be experienced because it is in the experience of it that we are truly changed by the encounter. This is how we gain understanding. The truth that we have encountered has physically become a part of our own being. We become truth and it is that truth that we have become, that sets us and others free.

Many years ago, as I struggled through another level of freedom, I asked God that age old question: "Why?" Why me? Why so much pain and hardship? Why, why, why? He answered my questions in an unusual way. I want to share this with you as an example of how I receive understanding. In Luke 10, Jesus appoints seventy-two disciples and authorizes them to go in teams of two to the surrounding towns he was going to visit himself. They went ahead of him, and he gave them specific instructions on what to do and not do on their journey as his ambassadors. In verse 17 they return to him with great joy over what they had seen and done on his behalf. They were in awe that demons had obeyed them! Jesus basically says, "Hey, listen. I saw Satan himself fall from Heaven like lightening. You are focused on the wrong thing here. The fall is not what is a big deal. It is the authority that caused that fall that matters. I have given you my own authority. The really big deal is that this authority is not just backed by my name, but your name speaks from Heaven, too!"

This story has been told countless times to encourage us to battle demons. But Luke 10:20 struck me: "...rejoice that your names are written in Heaven." Why is that a bigger deal than having Satan and demons submitting to us? What is Jesus pointing to? I meditated on this visually, diving deeply into that story and asking what it meant. I dove into the study tools determined to understand it better. The Lord answered me in that exercise. He told me that when I beat a demonic stronghold in my own life by obtaining the victory that Jesus died and bled for me to have, I become authorized as a legal weapon in Heaven against that demonic entity in the Earth. Every victory I win is a victory Jesus already obtained for me. But when I become one with that victory, it changes my legal record in Heaven and in the Earth! My name is registered in the spirit realm and economy as a gun would be in the Earth. I am registered against sexual abuse, eating disorders, depression, suicide, emotional and physical abuse...and so much more. The cost was great, but the real truth is that His blood purchased my testimony, not just my freedom. So, if someone around me is going through what I went through and it must cost them the same price that I paid, I have not done my job. I have not used my authority, or I am empty of bullets to be used against those beings influencing their life.

How important is it for you to recognize that you belong to an incredible family whose origin and power are spiritual in nature? Everything we do as God's children has the potential for great harm to his enemies. The authority that we have from Jesus is meant to be a starting place for so much more. He wants us to do so much more than just beat demons down. He wants us to set people free with authority we have gained by partnering with him to our own account. Your name has a record attached to it in Heaven. Hebrews 12:23, Psalm 87:6, and Isaiah 4, all speak of a Heavenly record. There are also several references to our names being in the Book of Life or the Lamb's Book of Life. The statement Jesus made to the disciples about rejoicing that their name and his, was meant to help them understand the weight of their actions.

They were not just dispelling demons, but they were building their testimony. That is where the power of Jesus' name and the power of your testimony connect. He won, so you could win too! Our greatest privilege is to undo the work of the enemy in the lives of other around us, so they too can set others free.

I would say that if you don't dare to grasp this truth you will be only gain access to freedom through the offerings that this natural realm offers. As a counselor myself, I can say that the best counseling in the world will take time to set you free. But there is a multiplied power of faith available when a spiritual brother or sister who has gotten a revelation that their Father loves them and has authorized them in the rescue of others. This knowledge of victory and freedom stemming from a place of entitlement is powerful. If you have been set free from a bondage, then you know what I mean. To undo the work of death and sin in the life of another person from a place of realized entitlement is intoxicating. We are not trying to be powerful or holy. We are. We are constrained to the likeness of God in the spirit. We are children set free from sin, to sin no more.

To be powerful and engaging in the spirit realm as if our eternal nature were right now victorious over all the works of the enemy is our foundational truth. Do you believe it is for freedom you have been set free or are you still fighting a losing battle against your flesh? Do you know that you have a family meant to support you? Have you shared your struggles with someone else? Are you tapping into your family's potential?

Even more compelling is the fact that your enemy has no power to withstand the nature of your family name. Jesus is the pinnacle, author and perfector of this faith life. His name literally means, deliverer or one who comes to the rescue. He is the first and greatest. He wants you to continue the family legacy of deliverance. It is time for you to come to the rescue of someone else. May your name and testimony destroy the work of the enemy in someone else's life. May you be that lethal weapon in the hand of the Lord on the Earth! Why are we are waiting for God to do the greater things through us, while He is waiting for us to notice him in others. Your miracle has hands and feet. They are alive right now on the Earth or soon to be born.

God has taken up residence in man (Eph. 2:5; Col. 2:13) and obtains victory over his enemies – person to person. Family to family we are irrevocably linked to the power of each other. In the moments when we come alongside of others in their pain and listen, encourage and pray for them, the chest of God as a father is pumped up with pride! He created us to be moved with compassion, like Jesus was in scripture. He designed and built us with the tools to deal with hard things and effect change on the Earth. When we work together to help each other change and grow, we are doing the "greater works" that Jesus said we would perform on the Earth (John 14:12). We make that greater work too much about a new kind of miracle. Sometimes the small acts of showing up for people when they are stuck in ugly and can't figure out how to get back up from a fall is a miracle for them!

When that happens, I call it the "footstool effect" from Hebrews 10:13 and Romans 8:34. declares that Jesus is seated at the right hand of God, making intercession for us and waiting until his enemies become his footstool. This is not a fluffy upholstered stool under Jesus' feet! The word *until* there is the Greek word "heos"[13] which means to mark in a sense of the end of an allotted timeframe. Mark the end of what? Oh!!! - The footstool moment. This word *footstool* is the word, "neuter"[14] in the Greek. We know what it means to neuter an animal. Luke, the author, literally means - *until the organs that cause propitiation of the cycle are cut off and have come to an end in terms of purpose and function.* Jesus is waiting until you prove by your own victories in life that your entire family has the same rights! Sorry to be so graphic but let me say it this way. A neutered dog cannot reproduce after its own kind any longer. So why on Earth is the world so in bondage to sin? The family of God does not understand how well-positioned we are to live free and powerful lives, nor how much authority we must enact freedom for others! Instead, many choose to suffer alone, hide their struggles, and pretend to be something they really can't back up inside.

God designed his children to rise together! To bear with each other and call each other up into the glorious liberty of a life lived with him (Gal. 6:2). Do you know who your family is? Do you have a spiritual family? People who will pray with you and walk with you as you struggle against temptation. Is there a group of people who see you not as a sinner saved by grace but a son or daughter saved from sin to do great and glorious things on the Earth?

Do you know how you can tell if someone is your family or not? If I were to ask them to tell me about you, they would share the best parts of you and regale me with stories of the things you escaped from or the exploits you performed. They would be proud of you. They would know you in such a way that I could discover you through their own experiences with you. This is family. This is the framework for the Kingdom of God. It is not always pretty, or all perfectly cleaned up. Yet it touches God's heart as a father when we are transparent in order to help each other out. This is what the church of Acts 2 was built upon – knowing the needs of others and meeting them in such a way that the entire community was strengthened and grew. The "Church" was a family then and still is now. We are God's family, and it is when we abide together in the hard places that we grow stronger and truer as a reflection of God's glory together. We do hard things, together! That should be the mantra of every group of Christians.

In this era of technology, we have even more opportunity to communicate about needs and challenges, as well as celebrate births and promotions. I believe an online group of people can be as intentional to parent children, raise young adults, bear with families and individuals in victory and loss, and still be a great family. It is not so much that we have to physically live together. I am as close to my daughter today as I was years ago when she lived with me. In some ways we are even closer. But she is married and living in another home in another state.

Yet, when we pray together or talk about challenges, or support each other in need, we feel the love and affection of a mother and daughter "seeing" each other. I am intentional about connecting with her. There are people I call family who live in other states, even countries! They are often the person I call when I need prayer or want to celebrate something amazing. With so many people being motherless or fatherless in our country, we as ministry-minded people need to understand that the church is not a building with a roof and walls. It is a collaboration of effort between people who have covenanted to see, know and love each other.

I remember a woman in my early 20s who was a clinical instructor at my nursing school. I was in school learning to be a licensed practical nurse. It was my ticket out of poverty and I worked hard at it. I had a full-time job as a nurse's aide and often went to work after school on the same floor that I had done clinical in the shift prior for school. I had two small children and an absent husband. It was a tough life, but I was fighting with everything I had to try and prove I could do something different with my life. Remember that boots straps mentality I mentioned? It was in high gear! During that time, this instructor was particularly hard on me. She was constantly asking me to demonstrate something for the class in clinical and would, in my humble opinion, correct me harshly before the class. I was fed up one day and probably emotionally exhausted, and so I yelled out to her, "Why are you so mean to me and always asking so much of me?"

She answered me without a hesitation. "Because you are better than this. You should be in RN school, not LPN. You are too smart and gifted to be doing a half-ass job at something you can do easily." I remember in that moment how shocked I was. I had never had anyone acknowledge what I secretly sensed inside of myself. I was really smart. I could do really big things with my life because of it. I was better than what I was attempting to do. The day I took my boards for the LPN license, I walked out of the building with everyone around me crying and talking about how hard it was. I was silent. Inside I knew I had passed the boards. It had not been hard for me at all. My instructor was right. I still remember her name today. Even though she was tough and hard, she was the first person that affirmed what I suspected inside. I was destined for more. Her candor and push were a form of parenting for me. She re-parented that broken girl in that moment who had been treated so carelessly and caused her to begin to believe that maybe she might be something special. Thank you, Ann!

In my life, I have had the privilege of mothering many spiritual children and pouring into their lives. They have grown under my care and shared hard things with me. Some now even support me as adults when I experience hard things. My sons and daughters pray for me before I minister, share words of prophecy with me, helped me pack to move, and in general have blessed me in countless ways. I did not pour into them because I wanted something in return. I wanted them to experience what I never had.

Though the Earth is full of coaching and mentoring movements, I believe God's heart is that we would see those who are fatherless and motherless. Wandering aimlessly and needing direction and encouragement, deliverance, and healing, these are the moments where our hearts can be moved with compassion like Jesus was. I want to parent those who did not have parents. This can be a natural condition related to the pains of their past or a spiritual condition related to the confusion of life now or the lack of a future hope. I want to leave this Earth with a legacy of sons and daughters who grew closer to the Father, knew themselves better, and experienced that unconditional love He has shown me. I want to be known as a Lady Wisdom, that I shared knowledge but more so, that I fostered an understanding of the power of family.

I pray that you catch the heart of this and begin to look around you for those God is asking you to call family. This is the moorings of the move of the Church on the Earth, and we are not too far gone to reclaim it. Time spent with others as they find their way often softens the pain of the adversity they may be experiencing. In this way we abide together with them in pain and hence reap the reward of their freedom and the great things they do with that freedom. We foster wisdom in and for them. Even more compelling, we can create space for understanding in their own lives. And the reward of that is to our account, not just theirs!

Life Application

1. What truth has God revealed to you as wisdom? Share one.

2. Have you pursued it unto understanding? Show how that truth has been experienced in your life and become understanding.

3. Have you stewarded by sharing it with another person?

4. What specific authority do you have personally because of the victories you have won with God's help in your life? Make a list. That is your armory!

5. Take some time to write down a list of the questions you have for God. Then offer them in prayer to him. Ask him not just for the answers but for the understanding of it so that you might experience it and share it with others.

Chapter Ten
ABIDING WITH PAIN

Abide within as I abide in thee. Though all else change, in Me remain. Be steadfast, true, find Me. And when you find Me, remain.

—From My Personal Journal

John 15 is one of the most amazing chapters in the Bible! I don't think Jesus could have painted a clearer picture about what his relationship with his Father was like.

I am the true vine, and my Father is the gardener. He cuts off every branch in me that bears no fruit, while every branch that does bear fruit, he prunes so that it will be even more fruitful. You are already clean because of the word I have spoken to you. Remain in me, as I also remain in you. No branch can bear fruit by itself; it must remain in the vine. Neither can you bear fruit unless you remain in me. "I am the vine; you are the branches. If you remain in me and I in you, you will bear much fruit; apart from me you can do nothing. If you do not remain in me, you are like a branch that is thrown away and withers; such branches are picked up, thrown into the fire and burned. If you remain in me and my words

> *remain in you, ask whatever you wish, and it will*
> *be done for you. This is to my Father's glory, that*
> *you bear much fruit, showing yourselves to be my*
> *disciples. "As the Father has loved me, so have I*
> *loved you. Now remain in my love.*

—**John 15:1-9** (NIV)

There is a principle of abiding that is deeply captured by this picture. In South Africa, I had the
opportunity to stay in a home nestled amongst fields of
grape vines. I never once saw a vine growing wild on
the ground with fruit on it. They were all propped up
and fixed with a vantage to the sunshine. It was obvious to me that the tending of grapes is a very detailed
business. They are supported from the time they are put
into the ground as a young stalk. The more fruit they
bear, the more support they require. The fields of vines
were a network of wood, string and a variety of other
factors all intertwined for one purpose - the growth of
grapes. The highest quality of grape is produced by the
most closely and carefully tended vines. The oldest
amongst these are considered very expensive in value.
But the gardener, as Jesus pointed out in his story, has
the most important job. It is his responsibility to know
the state of all of his plantings.

Jesus said bearing much fruit is reliant upon one important factor - remaining in him. We are the branch,
but he is the source vine itself. Without him we can do
many things but he said in verse 5 that it amounts to
"nothing". Your fruit in the Kingdom is particular to

your own part of the vine. So many of us are trying to bear fruit like others. But the vinedresser or gardener is the one who assesses the fruit of its branches as worthy of the vine he planted. I don't want to be worthy of bearing someone else's fruit. I want to be pleasing to him and bear the fruit he designed my life. And then there is a big "ouch!" in verse 2.

Even when you bear fruit according to your structure and purpose, he still prunes you! How many times in your life have you been doing what you thought was the best job ever at something you were doing for the Lord – being a mother, or father, a student, a worship leader, a market-place leader or a cashier with joy on her face. Then all of a sudden, the season changes and the life you have been living seems to have come to an end. Even if your feet are still in the same place, your hands still moving the same items across a conveyer belt, your mouth still preaching the word of God, it feels like bitter grapes. Or perhaps the season ends because you just lost your audience, your job, your relationship. At these moments we cry out, tears flow, and rage becomes our friend. In that bitter place, we start to retract inward and question God. We cry out in anger, "Why is this happening to me? I was doing exactly what I was supposed to do. And I was doing it well! Why am I under attack?!"

That cry is exactly what the gardener is after. A branch that has been cut begins to dig down towards the roots again for sustenance. The truth of pruning is that the life-time of the vine is determined not by its fruit but by its pruning process. It needs to be cut in order to grow after a fruitful season. Allow me to share with you a particular cutting process. A shallow cut is performed in a perfect circle just through the bark of the vine towards its top. They then peel the bark back just a bit to get it started. Gradually all of the outer bark comes off the vine from that point, all the way down to the soil. It is painful looking as it curls up and falls away like dead skin. Yet, this process is essential to the vintner. If he wants the vine that produced the best grapes last year, to do even better next year - either by producing more flavor or more grapes - than the vine itself must be strengthened. This process of "girdling" the tree so that it almost seems to die as it sheds its skin is performed during the winter months when the fruit bearing branches are bare. There is nothing to support, and so the process itself causes the branches of the vine to turn inward and dig down into the root system for more sustenance. It not only furthers the root system during what would be a hibernation season, but it also thickens the trunk of the vine itself as it grows. At the end of the process, the vine has more strength in the trunk, a larger root system to sustain the entire vine and more fruit-bearing capacity. If they are really good at it, the grapes themselves will not only be more plentiful but be even tastier. This is all thanks to the painful process it has been through.

There is a grief that is to be expected when we experience pruning. I don't think we talk about that enough. We are fine with the tears of someone who lost a valued member of their family, but we are uncomfortable with the weeping that comes from the loss of a job or an opportunity or a relationship. "Stop crying over spilt milk!" We make light over what is essential to our process. With grief comes healing. The vine that has been cut weeps on purpose. If God created a plant to weep than why are we so uncomfortable with the weeping of loss? If you can give room for grief however it comes, you can allow your grief to turn into acceptance. In acceptance you can find new vision for your life. There are things God wants to say to you that He can't say the same way until you have been pruned, weeping and leaning into Him closely, as if your life depended on it. Listen to me. It does! Your spiritual DNA is tied to the gardener's love for you. His tending of you is in light of your lifetime. Longevity and fruitfulness are his passion. Abundance is his heart. Grace is his secret weapon. Mercy is his shade by day. Comfort is his cloak of protection in the evening. Loneliness is never meant to be your companion, because your gardener is also the source of your root's irrigation system. The soil of his word is enriched and turned over until the right conditions are there for you to draw upon.

When I lost a relationship that was very dear to me recently, I wanted to die in the initial days of its loss. It was a complicated and painful situation. It hurt, even when I captured a scent of freedom that begged me to follow it. My fixer mode felt handicapped, my tongue tied and my face frozen. Even when the scent of freedom came, I could not allow myself to follow it with my heart. My mind and heart felt disconnected. I wanted to give myself the gift of understanding and when I couldn't find it, I just gave in to sorrow. I felt like a boat set adrift in an ocean without a functional engine or an anchor to stem my progress. The further I was carried from the initial events, the more lost

I felt. Others would come and row my boat for a while and help me to make sense of the day I was in, but the overall direction of my life was being so radically changed that I felt like I had been captured by a rip current. When I gazed behind me there was no land left in sight. I could not see the life I had been living nor plot a course to go back to it.

God's hand of restraint was on me to keep me from going backwards. He then graced me with a few prophetic words from men of God who did not know anything about my circumstances but spoke into them powerfully by God's Spirit in those days. When the Bible says that the word of the Lord runs swiftly when it is released in order to perform what it was sent for (Psalm 147:15), that was true in my life in those days. I felt like the words themselves were having their way. They were a current like that rip tide pulling me away from the dysfunctional relationship I had grown used to, comfortable in. Even when I wanted to go back, the current carried me further away. I cried buckets of tears, wailed like someone had stolen my child, and at times, just slept without dreams.

The word of the Lord to me protected from future pain and harm, and it pulled me away from going back. The words I shared in the preface of this book also came then, concerning having global citizenship and traveling the world. They beckoned to me and destroyed my nesting and sleeping patterns. Though I wanted to bury my head like a mole in the ground, faithful friends pulled me out and stayed with me as I grieved, dreamed, and then wept some more. The prophetic words about ministering to people globally began to show up in my dreams as the voices of men and women I had not yet met from other countries became compelling and pulled to me with promises of encounters I could barely remember when I woke. This book title was spoken in one of those prophetic words - Faith, you are not normal. Like the title of this book, I was discovering just how un-normal I was. God wanted me to know that this was truly the purpose of my life – to raise a standard over God's family that celebrated the unique individuality of each and every person as an expression of his glory on the Earth. To create a movement that would champion the heart of God for family where people would learn to be interlaced heart to heart, story to story until the entirety of all the notes of music and sound we each make is a finished song, just as it was in God's heart.

To be un-normal is to be atypical, unable to be identified by a type, group or class. It is to be fully, uniquely you! When we all embrace this, there is a beautiful sound that I am convinced is as a symphony being played before all of Heaven's courts! It delights God's heart in its sound!

I climbed out of my pain day by day with the incredible help of friends and spiritual parents. My family of faith was amazing! God brought even my natural family around me though they had been very distant for most of my life, and friends ministered to me daily. I was not alone in my pain. I was with others who shared my pain with me and led me through that sense of disorientation by pointing me over and over again towards God and his promise of a certain good future ahead. (Jeremiah 29:11)

The pain we often feel in life is part of the process of life itself. Yet, Hebrews 12:2 tells us something so amazing! For the joy that was set before Jesus, He endured the cross and despised not its shame! His endurance gained him the joy of being with his Father again. Not as He was before, but with us in his plan. We are his joy! Yet, in this scripture we see a holy exchange took place. As he endured pain, he did so with joy in the cross hairs of His scope of vision. He invites us into that same joy today. There is nothing he has gained that we have not been invited to experience for ourselves. We can burrow into him in these moments of pain and find a supernatural supply of his own joy, just as he did when facing the cross.

What does that look like? Well, it depends on what you are going through. I once saw a young pregnant mother sing a worship song for everyone at her own husband's funeral with joy beaming from her face even as family and friends sat weeping before her. It makes my hair stand on end every time I remember it. I didn't understand it. I didn't need to. Her pain was not mine to bear. But I know this. Her joy in those moments changed me forever! I sat in her presence as part of her family of faith supporting her and being forever changed by her legacy of honor at the same time. Thank you, Rita. Your song to the Lord that day reminds me today that he is faithful! The courage of your grief and joy in those moments are forever imprinted on my heart and soul for reference.

Better than any substance we might be afforded on this Earth, any pill, program, or truth, is the knowledge that no one will ever understand our process like God. So why not talk to Him? The Psalms are full of David's outpouring of his pain and his delight in God. It is hard to experience one without the other. So, cry out to God and let yourself begin to dig deep into the roots of God's love for you found in the vine - Jesus. If even he had a cry of agony in the Garden of Gethsemane, do you really suppose he might be surprised by your own? Remember, he desires to afford you all that helped him to accomplish his own hard task so you can experience a new kind of garden living. If you are in a season of pruning and find yourself fighting it, start digging down. Get really honest with God. Don't offload your pain or lack of vision by getting busy with whatever mission is next in the lives of others. Go to your Designer. He alone can show you the fruit of what seems like loss in the pruning season. He will, in such a way, that you may forget to regret what you lost.

Life Application

1. What is God pruning from your life?

2. Have you experienced the joy that the author describes? If so share it with the group.

3. What has the Lord shown you about your future that you've yet to experience?

4. Grief and joy are both very vibrant feelings and experiences. They require us to lean into them in order to grow through them. Is it hard for you to associate growth with these? If so, why?

5. What does your own support system look like in your pruning seasons? Ask God for family if you feel unsupported. He places orphans (lonely people) in families. Its his promise! (Psalm 68:6)

Chapter Eleven
GARDEN LIVING

Now the Lord God had planted a garden in the East. And there he put the man He had formed.

—Genesis 2:8

God has always had a garden lifestyle in mind for mankind. It must have been a pretty amazing place for Adam and Eve. There they could have anything – but one thing. They had all of life, all of God, relationship with each other and the created world around them. So much to keep them busy, but the enemy always has a way of causing us to think that even in the midst of abundance, we are missing out on something. That something else you need can be the breeding ground of discontentment. Pursuit of it will not only lead you into sin, but also into idolatry. You risk sacrificing the blessings of your life on the altar of having more. This is the true bondage of life - to give away our gift of life for that which we were never designed to gain or sustain. For whatever you gain with your flesh alone, your flesh will have to sustain, alone.

Monet, a famous impressionist painter, painted gardens to serve as a haven of peaceful meditation for people who viewed them. His artwork is like taking a vacation into a place we wish we could be. If you pause for a longer moment with his art, you will find your imagination taking you there. You can smell the roses and other fragrances that fill the air. You can sit on a bench and admire it as the wind blows upon the garden, inviting you to stay and live there. We were designed by God for garden living. Our senses come alive and begin to interact with each other; inviting us to remain and be one in the garden's experience with life.

This desire to abide is birthed out of this reality. I don't think it is a mistake that Jesus retreated to a garden nestled amongst an olive grove in Gethsemane. I recently had the opportunity to visit an olive grove in South Africa. It was so beautiful! The trees are light and filled with feathery leaves; the olives vary in shades of ripeness upon the trees. They hide amongst the leaves so that you almost have to look for them hidden on the trees. I can imagine they feel the leaves are like a safe covering. And yet, I also believe the olives were a poignant reminder to Jesus in that olive grove called, Gethsemane, that his body was about to be crushed with pain and torment like those olives would be crushed to extract their precious oil. His life blood would be poured out for us.

Mature olive trees have the most interesting boughs. They are wizened with age and seem to have taken turns in their growth process to avoid something we can't see on the surface. They have knots and turns, and yet they continue to produce the fragrant oil from those olives, year after year. Olive oil is first bitter and its fragrance earthy and biting in your nostrils. As it matures in a bottle, it widens its bouquet. When filtered, its purity is so light that you can use it for a variety of purposes. It maintains its clarity and temperature better than any other oil. Only a true olive grower will tell you this. It is healthier for you and easier to fry with than every other oil because it can sustain such a high heat in its purified state.

The pure sacrifice of Jesus Christ on the cross has released a clarion anointing for those who walk in His footsteps that is powerful, light and makes everything easier to bear. Yet, like those olives and like Jesus, we must go through the pressing to become acquainted with this other way of life. The older I get, the more I am convinced that garden living is the only way we can hope to go through this life and be fragrant no matter what comes our way. Like every garden plant, we are called to go through stages of growth and development. Not to harm us but to develop within us the Christ-life in such a way that we would be compelling to the world around us.

These stages are meant to draw out our fragrance. 2 Corinthians 2:15-16 details this fragrance as being the fragrance of life to those seeking life but the scent of death to those who are not! The more our fragrance is filtered by the process of maturing and growing in God, the higher the grade of heat we can bear up under. The clearer the oil of the anointing on our life, the less it smells like the additives of our human sins and faults. Garden living creates a cycle of life that causes us to be more and more like our Father's design.

Have you ever wondered what it was like for Adam and Eve to be "with" God in the garden of Eden? The details have been written about and summaries surmised by many scholars and theologians. I love how Genesis 3:8 details what Adam and Eve experienced in the garden in their new fallen condition. They heard the "sound" of God walking in the "atmosphere of the day." Their eyes were blinded as they hid in their fallen condition and spiritual death, but their ears could still hear the sound of God coming in the garden. Maybe they saw the garden itself responding to that sound. However, it was experienced by Adam and Eve, it frightened them. They hid themselves from God. Sin always tries to get us to hide from sight! God asks them, "Where are you?" Adam responds by talking about his fear over his newly discovered naked condition. What an interesting response. He had lost something that he once had. To be naked is to be void of covering. Nakedness in itself is not evil or shameful. Surely Adam had named many such "naked" creatures? In the same token, we are not told what Adam and Eve lost that exposed their nakedness to them. Perhaps it was not what they lost that mattered. It was the knowledge they had gained.

In eating of the one forbidden tree in the garden they had gained knowledge. The words of the enemy proved to be true, to a degree. They gained a knowledge of their condition which God was aware of. But without his immutability they had been changed by that knowledge. It was not in their design to know such things. Hence, the knowledge separated them from God and from each other. Separation became part of their equation and they dealt with it by making clothing out of fig leaves. The separation made them suddenly feel very vulnerable, even unsafe. They felt the need to cover up and hide.

We know the rest of the story. Adam blamed Eve. Eve blamed the serpent. The serpent received a new low condition without even an opportunity to defend himself. Interestingly, God refused to do what Eve did. He never engaged the serpent in conversation. He simply arraigned him and gave a judgment based on his crime of influence. Both Adam and Eve's verdict is one based upon their new separation from the realm of God. Not only would they live a life that led to death, but they would live a natural life void of the eternal benefits of the immortality of the spirit realm. The Earth, the womb and the grave would become harsh companions for them.

God's final act was to cover their naked human forms with skin. Though many have told the story of the first blood shed by God having been to cover them with the skin of an animal he had killed, the Bible does not depict that. He simply made for them the same type of covering called "skin" that we wear today until we yield to death. Their spirit and soul were encased in mere humanity. Their unhindered access to the freedom and life-giving youth of the spirit realm would no longer be theirs. God would come to them. He would come upon men and women in the ages to follow. But it wasn't until the resurrection of Jesus that he would once again gain access to humanity in a relational way. We would become children with nothing in between us. He did so in such a way that he places his own DNA in the form of a seed - the Christ seed - into each person who called him Father and received the gift of having their storyline embedded with the story of Jesus the Christ. The bearer of the first seed has a story that has been told within his own blood that is so detailed that were you to visit it forensically you would discover so much. It tells the story of all things you have been forgiven of that you had not even performed yet. The power of that invasion in your storyline takes place in seed form first. But it is meant to grow into a tree and bear fruit.

We are garden dwellers, yes! But even more so, we are those who are trees of life. I believe trees are significant of the children of God. Revelations 22:2 tells of trees who line the streets of the city of Zion. All accounts of life after death include a story of a garden. The new Zion in scripture is mentioned even in the stories of those who have died physically only to return to their mortality. How can we hope to understand the nature of our life-giving force if we refuse to take our place in the garden? The garden represents life and contains all the creatures, seeds, herbs, and naturally growing substances that bring life not only to us but to others. The leaves on those trees in Revelations 22 are good for healing. I am taking olive leaf ground into a powder in a capsule form to right some imbalances in my internal systems currently. Have you ever thought that your own being was meant to be like those leaves I am taking as supplements? That your life can heal the life of others? How would we develop if we were to embrace this garden living?

Scripture very clearly encourages us about our lives being like a garden in Isaiah 58:11, Isaiah 61:11, and

Luke 13:19. John 15 is an entire description of how to look at life in light of being garden dwellers. Perhaps we are more like Adam and Eve's original design right now, than we realize! Is it possible that because of our new life in Christ that our skin suits are not as limiting as we have thought? I don't think we have a hope of understanding this unless we take up the art of abiding, as Jesus did. In our abiding with God as Jesus did, so many unusual things can happen!

I once studied pollination in plants. The goal of every living organism God created, including plants is to create offspring for the next generation. Pollination is the process by which a plant fertilizes itself or another plant in order to propagate. Water, wind and insects provide stimulation that carries what is in one plant into another so that it might be pollinated or fertilized and thereby produce new seed and fruit. ***Somehow, as we abide together with God, and with each other, we are pollinated, or stimulated to produce.*** Our garden living, according to Matthew 12:35 produce good things out of our good heart.

This is part of why isolation is the enemy's tactic to keep us from engaging when we are hurt. God designed us to be relational beings. However, because we have often been hurt in relationship or through it, unhealthy habits or defense mechanisms litter our garden life. These dysfunctional relationships further pollute rather than pollinate. God wants to deal with the pollution, so we don't lose our ability to be stimulated and cross pollinated by the good things stored up in the heart of others.

These good things are more than just mere knowledge, or skillsets. The power of God is in you to change the lives of others! A few years ago, I was sitting in a service waiting for it to end. I was overtired and wanting to go home to sleep. As the service ended, a young woman came to the front looking for our pastor to pray for her for healing. She was in excruciating pain from a fall down her cellar steps. She had come to service and stood in the back of the sanctuary with her mind set that she would receive healing from her Pastor after service. He had an appointment after service and was not available, but I was. She asked me to pray for her.

Even as I said yes to her, I reasoned with the Lord in my mind, "Do you know how tired I am? How will I muster faith for this woman who is obviously in so much pain?" I heard in my spirit the passage from James 5:14 where we are instructed to go to the elders of the church and they will lay hands on us, anointing us with oil, for healing. I walked to the place where we stored a small vial of oil for this purpose and as I came back rubbing my hands together, I used that time to place my faith in the word of God. I was an elder, and I had anointing oil. She would be healed. But in my humanity, I felt nothing special, not even compassion for her. I was too tired. I laid my hand upon her back, and she moved it down to the spot where the pain was the most severe. As she did so, a sensation of extreme heat hit my hand. It was as if I had touched a hot iron! I let out a brief sound of shock as I pulled my hand off her back. It was my hand that was hot! The heat was there but the pain left my hand, and I placed it back on her back. I then felt led to place my other hand on her abdomen. I prayed briefly in the spirit and then commanded her back to be healed. The entire prayer took less than 3-4 minutes. I felt that heat emanating back and forth like an arch between my two hands. When the sensation of the heat dissipated, I asked her how she felt. She said it was better. The pain was gone. She hugged me and left.

Here is the most amazing part of this story. She contacted me later and said that as she undressed that night, she found that her belt would not slide out of her pants. It was literally melted to her pants by the heat emanating from my hands during that moment of healing. She sent me pictures of her belt, the pants with the leather and the material melted on both. That heat was not just a sensation of the spirit realm manifesting in the natural for me. It was an actual manifestation of the power of God to heal this woman. His compassion through me, met her faith for healing and drew power out of a tired earthen vessel to produce the fruit of healing in her body. She ran a marathon a few days later. She was healed indeed!

When you live a life from the reality that you are attached to God as a root system, abiding in an ecological system that is spiritual first and natural second, then you are always a part of God's purposes that can bear fruit in every season.

He will be standing firm like a flourishing tree planted by God's design, deeply rooted by the brooks of bliss, bearing fruit in every season of

> *his life. He is never dry, never fainting, ever*
> *blessed, ever prosperous.*
>
> **—Psalm 1:3** (TPT)

The cultivation of garden living takes time. For me it began with setting up regular times of devotion to the Lord. I would set aside a time in the morning to spend with him. I used a devotional; a Bible I could write in and a journal to take notes in. That habit became routine for me and I always set aside a space in my home for just this. At times it was just a table and chair in a corner, while at other times I have had a room dedicated to the pursuit of him. Over time as I allowed myself to give more and more of my life to him, I would meet with him at other times in the day. I gave up lunch breaks to sit with him. I would take the 30–45-minute drive in the car to work and worship or talk to him and practice listening for his response.

I journaled questions, skipped a line in the journal and then began to write what I heard him saying back to me. It was as if I lent the Spirit of God my pen and the right to use my own journal to reply. And he would! I loosened my grip on the idea that prayer was a special activity separate from spending time with him. I allowed him to have access to all my days and all my times. He would talk to me in movies - superhero movies became a way of explaining the supernatural to me. I would see in the daytime so much, that I would ask him to not dream at night. I just wanted to sleep! He honored that for some time and then I began to dream again. My dreams have always been significant to community.

My garden space is always being invaded by the wind of the spirit, the rain of the Word of God and the needs of others to be influenced or pollinated by what God has put in me. I have learned to expect it and encourage it. Jesus told a parable in Luke 13:19 about the Kingdom of Heaven being like a mustard seed. It is the smallest of seeds but when it is planted in a garden, it grows into a huge tree that even the birds of the air can build a nest in! In Matthew 17:20, Jesus likens faith the size of a mustard seed to having the capacity to cast a mountain into the sea with a mere command. Mustard plants are an invasive species in nature.[15] They only take 8-10 days to grow into a tree and can take over an entire acre in 6-8 weeks. The sheer capacity of the plant to pervasively invade a garden speaks to the power of faith. A command by a man or woman who has faith in God active inside of them is like a seed spoken into the wind. It produces a mighty harvest against which nothing else can withstand its ability to produce after its own kind. Even a mountain can be overtaken by the harvest from a seed!

Another famous garden story is found in Mark 11:12-25. Jesus is hungry and walks up to a fig tree expecting to pick a fig from it. The issue in the natural, is this. The moment Jesus wanted the fig was not the season for the tree to bear fruit. Yet, the response Jesus has to the tree does not seem to consider the current season of the tree. He curses the tree for not bearing fruit for him! Later when they walked by the tree, it was dead from the root up. The disciples were amazed at this. They had only traveled two miles from Bethany to Jerusalem and back, so it is likely it died in the same day he cursed it. This is a prophetic demonstration of the purpose of their journey that day. They were on their way to the temple, the place built to host the presence of God. Yet when they arrive, Jesus began driving out merchants who were doing business in the temple. They were selling merchandise meant to help the people to pay for God's favor. The place and people who represented what God had designed to pollinate the Earth with his glory had no fruit to offer him. Like the fig tree whose leaves are large and glorious looking, the temple was grand and beautiful. Remember this is the tree that Adam and Eve used to cover their nakedness! They are large leaves with a pretty curve to them. The Temple in Jerusalem was glorious but void of the fruit of God's purpose or presence.

I fear currently that too many churches and people have lives that appear grand and glorious, but when God reaches for fruit amongst them, there is none to find. The tree in Psalm 1:3 is a metaphor for the life of God's children who meditate on his Word, allow their roots to dig down deeply into the water of his love and encounter sustenance from the invisible realm of the waters of his spirit. Planted according to his design, bearing fruit in "every season of life." Never dry, never fainting, always blessed, always tipped towards the prosperity of growth.

I challenge you to examine your life for fruit. I was vulnerable enough to tell you my "belt-melter" story as it really happened. I was exhausted physically. But

God's power supply in me was strong. I was rooted in the fruit of garden living. The faith of the young woman for healing could put a demand upon me and receive fruit. Unlike the fig tree that appeared glorious but had no fruit to offer Jesus, I appeared weary, but I had fruit to offer another person. This life of overflow is for every single child of God. This is garden living. This is a place of peace and purpose in God that lifts you above even the most difficult of circumstances in life. We are the ones who can do hard things well.

May your garden life become so rich and fragrant that like bees drawn to an open flower to extract its pollen, others will be drawn to your life and discover what they so desperately need to be alive and growing, too!

Life Application

1. What habits do you have to encourage growth in your life?

2. Do you have a designated space to be with God away from everyone else? Even Jesus got away...could you?

3. Take a time to write a question or concern out to God. Then skip a line and begin to write his response to you. Your pen belongs to him at that moment so don't try to read it as you write. When you finish that part, read it back and then skip a line and respond to him. This is called responsive journaling and can be very fruitful in your relationship with God.

4. What area would you like to ask God to cultivate growth in?

5. How might he be cross pollinating you to seed this growth in someone else? Take a moment to reflect on how your actions might be helping or hindering someone else.

Chapter Twelve
UNNORMAL

We are engineered by his design; he molded and manufactured us in Christ. We are his workmanship, his poetry. We are fully fit to do good, equipped to give attractive evidence of his likeness in us in everything we do.

—**Ephesians 2:10** (TMB)

In my lifetime thus far, I have gone from self-hatred so deep I would reject my body, harm it with food and other substances, to a completely different state of being. I would love to say that I have a garden life that is completely free of weeds. I can't. I do have a vibrant spiritual life and value the incredible opportunities I have to interact with people on a regular basis. More than any other thing, I no longer have an identity crisis. This girl named Faith Allison by her mother, has grown into a woman who accepts and loves herself. I am forever discovering new ways to celebrate how unique I am. I do not follow the trends of culture in order to arrive with a predetermined mindset of acceptance.

As I write the last chapter of this book, I am approaching my 54th birthday. When I am interviewed, I am often asked how long I have been saved or had a relationship with Jesus Christ. I said a prayer of salvation at the encouragement of the Baptist church I was in when I was about 5-6 years old. I received a box of candy in return! There was not much fruit from that prayer in my life. Relationship with God was never introduced to me in a vital, tangible way other than presenting him as a judge who was watching my every move. I made a lot of wrong moves! My life's abuses and empty ways of doing relationship seem like they should have been too great to allow me to ever encounter the true living God in the way I am describing to you. But I have and continue to every single day! God's incredible grace demands that we have encounters with truth throughout our lifetime. John 8:32 declares that it is the truth that sets us free, and God has determined that we will know and encounter truth in our lifetime. In small ways and really big, life altering ways, I have met with God, heard his voice, recognized his whisper and learned the gentle nudges of his Spirit. I love truth in all the ways he comes to me. I continue to learn this even today. My life with God really took wings when I was in my early 30's. If I were to give you a private garden tour of my life then, you would have found it full of weeds. It had been pollinated by the pain of others, and it was full of poisonous plants that fed my body toxins daily. But the truth that I have found in God and his scriptures have set me free to experience beautiful garden living.

The Greek word for truth found in John 8:32 is "aletheia"[16] and it means to be completely revealed and made known, to be available to be seen and visible to all. There is a lot of rhetoric about truth these days. My

truth, your truth, truth is subjective, not absolute, rela-
tive... Here is what I know about truth after years of
learning and searching for truth. Only that which God reveals to you about yourself and himself is completely
trustworthy. In our society today we are too easily swayed
by messages from the media, politicians, and leaders in
today's culture, and even the eloquent tongues of incredible preachers on screens across the world. I have had
seasons of life where to the dismay of those around me, I
have disengaged from listening to the news or watching
TV. I limited my intake of Christian books, novels, and
even my favorite preachers and teachers. Why? Because
the condition of my life does not depend on those voices.
It depends upon the voice of God. My realities find their
source in God's mind and heart.

I remember one time, as I carried around a book by one
of my favorite authors, the Lord challenged me by saying
this, "You have more affinity for the method than you do
the messenger himself." I was like, "What?!" Because at
that time, my life was being lived at a pace according to
the demands placed on me by others I had given my word
to, I was trying to get wisdom by reading books and listening to podcasts. I could do that in between assignments,
listen to a podcast while exercising, and was often found
multi-tasking with an alarming degree of speed that
caused the heads of others to spin. Yet my own internal
sphere was feeling a void of connection with God, with
his wisdom and power. So, I began to search for it in others. That search would cause me to begin to mimic them -
their language, style, and way of speaking about God.

I want to return to the garden analogy one more time. There is a process in nature called cross pollination. This happens when a plant cross pollinates with another plant outside of its own species. Although there are times when this can be exciting, it can also yield some terrible results for the plant as a whole. After much wasted pollen in an attempt to mate, the plants pair and bears a new kind of fruit. But that fruit often lacks the fortitude and strength of the original plant's genetic DNA. As a result, it is susceptible to disease and often causes the plant to not bear fruit that is as palatable as it might otherwise. It can also bear fruit that is not seed bearing. Much like a seedless watermelon. I really enjoy those! So much easier to eat, right? Yet have you ever stopped to think about the perversity of eating something that has no seed in it to propagate after its own kind again? The plant becomes dependent upon others to force what is natural within God's plan. Everything God has created has the ability to bear after its own kind. Unless it is forced to seek out other sources than those naturally afforded to it. There, in those scenarios we see all kinds of special anomalies in order to have something that was not according to God's original design. Man's best attempt at mimicking God produces designs that do not need God, do not need to propagate, lean towards death, but are convenient and easily accessed. Pause a moment a read that again!

Remember that definition for truth? If you have encountered truth that brings freedom, it will always show you who you really are. God's truth is not about exposing darkness but revealing light! It opens up our eyes to see what is already true and does so in such a way that I can incorporate it into my life as part of my own identity. It shows you who you really are. That is the fruit of understanding.

Like God, I occupy the very thing I have come to experience, and it is now a part of me. It can be so compelling to count on others to teach us and train us. You can end up with tons of knowledge like me and even some wisdom to share with others in between it all. Yet, only understanding allows you to apply it to your own life. Understanding agrees with and applies to your identity. Understanding happens when truth aligns itself with the design of God in you - even if it is not apparent to you or anyone else on the outside right now. It opens up the truth of who you are to God in such a way that your entire being begins to submit to that truth. You are, as He is. Who you are, is what you do. The true bondage of life is to carelessly spend your life on that which you were not designed to sustain. I never want to discourage people from learning. Yet, I do want to warn you that there are many voices to teach you and so much of what they say is laden with opinions. Too many people are but echoes of those they have learned from. I really tried to be true to scripture in this book. To bring to you the elements of the Word of God that have changed the way that I think about God, myself, and others.

1 Corinthians 4:15 carries a warning to us saying, "Though you may have 10,000 instructors in Christ, you do not have many fathers." Here is the truth of God's heart to us. He has designed us for family in a way that ensures

we are touched by Heaven's heart with a family touch. As compelling as a teacher's words may be to you, a father's hug will undo so much more in your life. The loving correction and affirmation of a true spiritual father or mother will teach you so much more than the doctrines or dictates of any religious movement full of the most educated scholars the Earth has to offer. Ultimately, civilization is crying out for family. It is the heart of God that we would propagate the Kingdom of Heaven with sons and daughters who have been lovingly taught to experience their identity in Christ.

Many years ago, I heard something that wrecked my heart. The Lord was saying to me that there are many great coaches and mentors in the movement called the Church today, but a mentor or coach at best can only reproduce after their own kind. They will teach you what they have learned and done. But God is not after cloning. He has designed each child so uniquely that they can't be recognized by just seeing their parents or their siblings. He is after spiritual parents - mothers and fathers in the faith - who will want for their children what they may not have experienced themselves. Only the heart of a mother or father would be willing to believe that their kids are extraordinary. To spend the time to know them like Paul knew Timothy, and Barnabas knew John Mark and Paul! To see their design and what they can't even see in themselves at times. Only a parent can love a child and believe in them so much that they would be willing to see them exceed even their own life and expectations. God is seeking those who will walk with his sons and daughters and coax them to stay engaged in the journey of healing and becoming. At times, we all need coaches to keep us from resting too long, but sometimes we also need a parent to guide us when we get too far off the road chasing after other things. What I lacked in my life; I became for others. I have no regrets there. I have lived long enough to have seen some of my children whom I lifted on my shoulders spiritually, now lift me and even exceed my own aspirations. I have sat and wept tears of joy in the audience as they lived out their dreams. Listen, this journey towards healing has not been pretty for me and I won't fail you by promising you it will be pretty for you, either. But in the messy trying, I promise you God will be with you and help you navigate everything – good, bad, and ugly! And he will send you people just like he has for me to walk with you and experience that sense of belonging that we all crave and long for in life.

These are the gentle rhythms of God's grace within his Body. This is the way of family in the Kingdom of God, and it takes time and commitment. It does not easily fit the patterns of the business realm or the marketplace models of today's culture. It honors every person as special and unique. It compels people toward change by championing what they already have within their design. It is not a harsh taskmaster beating the sin out of your life, but the loving touch of a father or mother encouraging you that you are better than appear to be.

Like stanzas in a poem or an orchestral composition being played a note at a time, we are all elaborately and yet simply designed to be brilliant, and significant to the entire working of God's message to the Earth. He is singing stanzas of songs of deliverance through our very life story. We are ambassadors of another Kingdom, an invisible realm, making known the mysteries of the DNA of God within these supernatural human forms. Whether we walk amongst the fallen or the celebrated of the Earth, we are ambassadors of God, who is making a plea through our lives. "Be reconciled to God through Jesus, the Christ that you might find your true redeemed identity" (2 Corinthians 5:20, The Mirror Translation). I am not the only unnormal person. We are all called to be unnormal; to go against culture's desire to put us in a box and label us. I call that "death in a box." We often live out of those boxes until we die with our callings and that which makes us glow with passion left untouched, nothing inspirational, or exceptional about us.

Our lives are meant to be a beacon of hope and potential to others. It doesn't mean we won't face hard things, but we never face them alone. All of Heaven is for us in this process we call life. The joy of becoming fully "me" is often painfully transformative and yet compelling at the same time. Each time I embrace another part of my design, I feel my Father's pleasure. I experience his power and purpose. I want the same for you. Listen, I have tattoos, a red faux- hawk hairstyle reminiscent of a decade ago and I dress a bit like a color dipped hippy at times! But I feel like me. Somehow those colors and the tattoo up my arms declaring, "I was made to love and to be loved" remind me of who I am to God. I was not made to be hidden away under layers of rejection, nor cookie cutter stamped in my Christianity. And neither were you.

We were made to be unNormal.

I pray that this book has inspired you to look around you for those you are called into family with. Remember there is not meant to be a short track to this. You won't be able to develop a system of relationship using a CRM or customer relationship manager on a computer. Facts are not relational. They come out of and serve relationship. They can help us be relational with people across the globe from us. But this kingdom work or method Jesus taught us will force us to slow down and get to know them deeper than what you see or what they allow you to see on the surface. More than anything I pray that this book helps you to embrace your own unique identity in God. May you reject all the messages that have labeled you but never fit you. May you seek out healing and make more room for truth in your life. Finishing well starts with taking one step, and then another. May you get on the road to naked, vulnerable living. Step out of the shadows and trust someone with your story as I have entrusted you with mine.

May you enjoy the journey to healing and see its process as beautiful and worthy of venturing on with God. May the seed of Christ in you that contains God's own DNA get to produce all of the fruit it was designed to grow in your life. May the Bible come alive in your life and be as a sword in your mouth. May your faith life be invasive in culture and may the Kingdom of God be expanded in your lifetime, and through the generations to whom you pass your inheritance. May you create a few "belt melter" stories of your own to share with others. Go do great things! I would love to hear about them!

You may email the author at hi@faithallison.com

UnNormal

UnNormal is BEAUTIFUL
Yes, it is true
For all who DECIDE…
I am **beautiful**, too

For the **broken** who wandered
Down the **crooked** path
On their way to wholeness
To find home at last.

For the **scarred** ones
The **proud** ones
The **bent** and **crazy**,

The **fiery** ones
With **burnout**
Yet embers still **blazing**

Called to stand out
Brave enough to be you.
To be **Seen**, **Known**, and **Loved**
To **BE UnNormal**, too.

©faithallison

References
NOTES

1. Skye, Jethani. *With, Reimaging The Way You Relate To God.* Thomas Nelson, 2011.

2. Strong's Concordance. Thayer's Greek Lexicon, Electronic Database. Copyright © 2002, 2003, 2006, 2011 by Biblesoft, Inc. All rights reserved. Used by permission. BibleSoft.com.

3. #5547 Strong's Concordance. Thayer's Greek Lexicon, Electronic Database. Copyright © 2002, 2003, 2006, 2011 by Biblesoft, Inc. All rights reserved. Used by permission. BibleSoft.com.

4. G1391 - doxa - Strong's Greek Lexicon (KJV)." Blue Letter Bible. Accessed 9 Jan, 2021. https://www.blueletterbible.org//lang/lexicon/lexicon.cfm?Strongs=g1391&t=kjv.

5. Lewis, C.S. *The Weight of Glory.* Harper, San Francisco, ©1949 C.S. Lewis Pte. Ltd., Copyright renewed © 1976, revised 1980 C.S. Lewis Pte. Ltd., pp. 45-46.

6. DuToit, Francois. *"The Mirror Bible,"* (note taken from THE MIRROR, Copyright 2012. Used by permission of The Author), 2018, page 43.

7. #266. Strong's Concordance. Thayer's Greek Lexicon, Electronic Database. Copyright © 2002, 2003, 2006, 2011 by Biblesoft, Inc. All rights reserved. Used by permission. BibleSoft.com.

8. Helps Word-Studies, Cognate: 1659. Copyright © 1987, 2011 by Helps Ministries, Inc. http://the discoverybible.com.

9. Helps Word-Studies, 1401-Doulos. Copyright © 1987, 2011 by Helps Ministries, Inc. http://the discoverybible.com.

10. Helps Word-Studies, 907-baptismo. Copyright © 1987, 2011 by Helps Ministries, Inc. http://the discoverybible.com.

11. DuToit, Francois. *"The Mirror Bible,"* (note taken from THE MIRROR, Copyright 2012. Used by permission of The Author), 2018

12. Matisse, Henry. http://www.matissepaintings.org/quotes/.

13. "G2193 - heōs - Strong's Greek Lexicon (KJV)." Blue Letter Bible. Accessed 9 Jan, 2021. https://www.blueletterbible.org/ /lang/lexicon/lexicon.cfm?Strongs=G2193&t=KJV.

14. "G5286 - hypopodion - Strong's Greek Lexicon (KJV)." Blue Letter Bible. Accessed 9 Jan, 2021. https://www.blueletterbible.org// lang/lexicon/lexicon.cfm?Strongs=G5286&t=KJV.

15. The Nature Conservatory. (22 July 2020). "Garlic Mustard: Invasive, Destructive, Edible." https://www.nature.org/en-us/about-us/where-we-work/united-states/indiana/stories-in-indiana/garlic-mustard/. Accessed November 15, 2020.

16. "G225 - alētheia - Strong's Greek Lexicon (KJV)." Blue Letter Bible. Accessed 9 Jan, 2021. https://www.blueletterbible.org//lang/ lexicon/lexicon.cfm?Strongs=G225&t=KJV.

ABOUT THE AUTHOR

Faith Allison is a pastor, teacher, trauma therapist, life coach, and author. She is a mother, grandmother and forever a daughter of the King of kings whom she lovingly calls "Poppa". She is an avid learner, a storyteller, and an advocate for the broken. She can be found walking with God in nature, along a beach or a winding path with her faithful dog Lucy Lou, or perhaps sipping coffee with a new friend. Life is a gift meant to be lived out loud to the glory of God's Kingdom family. She is busy living it to the fullest!

www.ingramcontent.com/pod-product-compliance
Lightning Source LLC
Chambersburg PA
CBHW051422090426
42737CB00014B/2785